THE WAY OF JESUS

COVERED IN THE DUST OF THE RABBI

MIKE MEGGINSON

Grace Lake
PUBLISHING

COPYRIGHT

The Way of Jesus: Covered in the Dust of the Rabbi
Publisher: Grace Lake Publishing (July 31, 2020)
Language: English
ISBN-13: 9780578677521
Original Copyright © 2020 by Mike Megginson
Editor: Stephanie Glines
Cover Design: Live Design
Formatting and Layout: Jason Garcia & Stephanie Glines
Printed in the United States of America.

CONTENTS

Special Thanks

First, I want to thank my home church, 3Circle Church of Fairhope, Alabama, for giving me and Sally the gift of two years of living on mission in Costa Rica. Without my church family, this book would not have been possible. I have had the honor of serving this local church for almost twenty-six years and it has been the most amazing ride of my life. They have taught me more about following Jesus than I have ever taught them.

I also want to thank our church family in Costa Rica, Iglesia Casa Vida. Thank you for trusting us and allowing us to do ministry with you. You guys are the real deal, Pura Vida!

I also want to thank our many supporters who have been standing shoulder to shoulder with us in your prayers and financial support during this time. Without you, we would not be where we are today. You have helped write this book.

I want to thank Chris Humphries for taking the time to correct my many mistakes.

Many thanks to Keith and Stephanie Glines for walking with me through the process of editing, formatting and publishing what you hold in your hands. They are an amazing team who love what they do.

Finally, I want to thank my family who has walked

with us and supported us through this adventure of faith. Lauren and Daniel, Leah, Daniel and Victoria, along with the most amazing grandchildren a "Papa" could have, you mean more to me than you know!

At the top of that list is my wife of 38 years, Sally, who sacrificed the most to follow this crazy idea to move to another country to do ministry. While most women her age are enjoying comfort and security, she was, well—not. None of our experiences and learning would have happened here without her faith and obedience to God's call: *"For where you go, I will go; and where you lodge I will lodge. Your people shall be my people and your God my God." (Ruth 1:16)* Thank you Sally for being my "Ruth" in all of our adventures together. I love you!

Author's Note

To my readers, I have to give you this initial disclaimer: I have never considered myself a writer and still don't! I have always been content to be a pastor and now a missionary who has spent the last two years living and working in Central America. Writing has only been a small blip on the radar screen of my life and ministry, casually considered, then quickly dismissed. I've always had this notion that the world is so full of books that there is really no need for one more from me.

Then I turned sixty last year. Age has a way of first catching you and then changing you—in many ways! So now, after thirty-plus years of life and ministry in the local church, I have arrived in a place where I have something that not only can be said, but to me, is actually something that *must* be said. What you hold in your hands is something that I felt compelled—even pushed—to give you that I hope will challenge and inspire you to rethink what it means to be a follower of Jesus. Of course, if you are reading this book and you are not yet following Jesus, my hope is that by getting to know him and his ways you will end up following him right along with the other 2.5 billion people around the globe who call him their Lord and Savior. That many people cannot all be wrong! My hope for you would be that from reading what you hold in your hands, you would be awe-struck with Jesus and that you would be compelled to follow him and trust him. I have no idea if I will ever feel the need to write again. Only the Father knows if I will or if I should. So, for better or for worse, I am going to give you all that I have. I hope that by the end of our time together on this journey, at the last page, in the last paragraph, with the last period, I will be empty, but you will be full. My hope and prayer is that, together, we will be following Jesus and becoming more like Jesus each and every day!

-Mike
Costa Rica 2017

Chapter One
The Way of Jesus

A disciple is not above his teacher, but everyone when he is fully trained will be like his teacher. (Luke 6:40)

Something has happened to the simple, yet radical and profound movement that was started 2,000 years ago by a Jewish carpenter from Nazareth. A movement that appeared to be dead on arrival with Jesus' crucifixion, in only a matter of days became a movement that would change the entire Roman Empire in the span of just 300 years. Since then, few would argue the fact that this movement has had a profound influence on the world as we know it to be.

But it seems to me and to many others here in the Western world, this movement that started with a roar has become merely a whimper of what Jesus intended. Sunday after Sunday, people gather together in large expensive buildings, sing songs, listen to a teaching, drop something in the offering plate, and then head out the door and on with their lives—merely checking a religious box on their ever-growing to-do lists.

Surely this cannot be the movement for which Jesus gave his life? Is this the movement founded on the wonder of a resurrected Christ? The movement that, within a matter of days, transformed Jesus' fearful disciples into fearless leaders who risked their lives to preach this message? The movement that swept across nations, that changed an empire, that shaped history, and for which countless faithful have given everything, even their own lives?

It cannot be. There has to be more.

A New Reformation

The book you hold in your hands is one feeble effort to help restart and reshape our thinking about what it truly means to be a Christian. I believe that what is needed and what is coming is a seismic shift in what it means to follow Jesus. You can think of it as a "new reformation." Just as Martin Luther poked his *Ninety-five Theses* into the eyes of a stale and corrupt Catholicism in 1517, there are more and more voices today who are calling for something just as radical. A reformation not of theology or knowledge or even of ecclesiology, but rather one of lifestyle, purpose, and mission.

This new reformation is calling us away from what some refer to as "Churchianity," with all of its shallowness and ineffectiveness, back to an ancient, authentic, revolutionary Christianity—a reformation that is once again rooted and grounded in the wildness and wonder of the person of Jesus.

Following Jesus

This new reformation is simply a response to an invitation from Jesus himself. Throughout the Gospels, the phrase Jesus most often used when he called out his disciples was "follow me." His encounter with Matthew was one of those times.

"As Jesus passed on from there he saw a man called Matthew sitting at the tax booth, and he said to him, 'Follow me.' And he rose and followed him." (Matthew 9:9)

It didn't matter that Matthew was a despised tax collector doing Rome's dirty work, padding his pockets with a little extra for his time and trouble. It didn't matter that he was considered one of "those people" by society. Jesus called him, and he followed.

So simple. So radical. Yet so utterly unlike the "Churchianity" of today.

One of the things I love about Jesus is that he always kept it simple. And in this complicated and chaotic world of smart phones and social media, simple is refreshing.

While following Jesus is simple, it's not without sacrifice. Throughout the Gospel accounts, Jesus warns that choosing to fully follow him will come at a cost.

"Then Jesus said to his disciples, 'If any of you wants to be my follower, you must give up your own way, take up your cross, and

follow me. If you try to hang on to your life, you will lose it. But if you give up your life for my sake, you will save it." (Matthew 16:24-25 NLT)

To "take up your cross" in that culture and context meant one thing, and that one thing was death. In other words, the invitation to follow Jesus is a death sentence to our selfish ways and to our agenda, in exchange for full and abundant life that only he can give.

German theologian, pastor, and Nazi dissident Dietrich Bonhoeffer, in his book *The Cost of Discipleship* said, "when Christ calls a man, he calls him to come and die."

Come and die. That's not a popular teaching in our churches today.

The call to follow Jesus is simple, but it is not easy. It will cost you. There will be a price to pay. But what object of value does not come with a cost?

I love being married to my wife, but it has cost me something (Of course, she would say that it has cost her more!).

I love my three adult children, but over the years, they have cost me something (Okay, they've cost a lot! My wife and I want to create a bumper sticker that says, "We could have been rich, but we had kids instead.").

I love my work, but it has come with sacrifice.

Following Jesus works the same way. There will be a price to pay. But if we accept his invitation, he promises that it will be more than worth it.

So, what does Jesus' invitation to follow him mean for

us today? Maybe the first clarification that needs to be made is what following Jesus does *not* mean.

- **Following Jesus is not about a set of rules and regulations or jumping through religious man-made hoops.** Although, as a Jewish rabbi or teacher, you would have expected Jesus to do just that. But Jesus refused to give us a set of rules. Instead, he reduced more than 600 Jewish rules and regulations down to just two: *Love God and love your neighbor.* That's what I would call de-regulation. Again, I love that Jesus kept it simple.

- **It's not about following a particular religion or about church attendance.**

- **It's not about following charismatic and gifted teachers and leaders.** Jesus skewered the religious leaders of his day by calling them "snakes," "white-washed tombs," and even "sons of the devil." How is that for winning friends and influencing people?

- **It's not about following your heart.** I hear people today say things like "just follow your heart." That may sound like good advice, even spiritual, but it's a dangerous notion. Jesus knew that what we refer to as the "heart" of a person could not be trusted. Scripture tells us the heart is deceitfully

17

wicked. Jesus knew that what we needed was a new heart that comes from a new birth and new life found in him.

True Christianity is about *following Jesus*. It's to lay down what we want, when we want it, and how we want it, and to take hold of what he wants. And what he wants from us is *everything*.

I love the ancient Jewish blessing that was spoken over young boys who were studying to become rabbis—"May you be covered in the dust of the rabbi." The original form of the blessing is found in Avot 1:4. *"Let your home be a gathering place for scholars, get dusty in the dust of their feet, and drink in their words with thirst."*

Surely this is a blessing that needs to be spoken over every believer—that we would be so closely following Jesus, we would be covered in his dust. That is the goal of the book you hold in your hands.

To Become More Like Jesus

Is there a point to this invitation to follow Jesus, other than one day going to heaven when we die? Actually, there is. The purpose of following Jesus is to become more like Jesus here and now.

Romans 8:29 says it like this:
"For those whom he foreknew he also predestined to be

conformed to the image of his Son, in order that he might be the firstborn among many brothers." (Romans 8:29)

Dear reader, think about the incredible truth of that verse. God knows you. He knows everything about you. Yet, God chose you in spite of everything he knows about you.

Growing up, did you ever have the painful experience of being the last one chosen for a team sport? You still remember the feeling of rejection, don't you? Well, God chooses you first for his team. In fact, Scripture tells us he chose you a long time ago, before the foundation of the world, to be exact. And in choosing you, it is true that God loves you just the way you are, but it is also true that he loves you too much to let you stay the way you are. God's plan for our life is for us to look like Jesus, live like Jesus, and love like Jesus. His plan is for you and me to be conformed to the very image of all that we see in Jesus.

It was C.S. Lewis who said in his classic, *Mere Christianity*, "Every Christian is to become a little Christ. The whole purpose of becoming a Christian is simply nothing else."

Regardless of your faith or lack of faith, your political persuasion, or what flavor ice cream you prefer, you have to admit that what we see of Jesus in the Gospel accounts is a model for the rest of us. If we could just live like Jesus lived, the world would be a much better place. Jesus was the guy who said things like "Turn the other cheek," "Love your enemy," and "Do to others as you would want them to do to you." He was the one who turned to the very people

19

who nailed him to a Roman cross and prayed, "Father, forgive them for they do not know what they are doing."

Whether you're a religious person or not, Jesus' impact on the world cannot be denied. It has now been more than 2,000 years and we are still talking, writing, and singing about this Jewish carpenter from a Podunk town in the middle of nowhere. And God's desire is for the lives of believers today to be just as impactful on the world around us.

Following Jesus to Become More Like Jesus

In a recent online article from 100movements.com, missiologist and visionary Alan Hirsch said, "Right now I would root our most fundamental dysfunction in our inability to recognize the Way of Jesus and to form our congregations in that Way. We just don't look like Jesus."

And that is the problem I see so often. We just don't look like Jesus. As a result, the Church has been weakened to the point of becoming irrelevant and impotent to be able to make any real change in its surrounding culture.

In his classic little book on revival, *The Calvary Road*, Roy Hession said, "The world has lost its faith because the Church has lost its fire."

For the Church, that fire is Jesus. It seems we are not following Jesus with the focus and passion needed to actually become more like him.

So, how does that change? How do we get started on this journey? How do we follow Jesus to become more like him?

First, there has to be a **commitment to follow.** Following Jesus doesn't just happen. You don't just wake up one day and discover that you are on your way. There has to be a commitment to get started. It is saying "yes" when Jesus calls "follow me." Have you done that? Have you said "yes?" If not, put the book down and just say "yes" to what you already know about following Jesus.

Second, there has to be a **change of direction.** You cannot keep going in the same direction and living the same way you have always lived and follow Jesus at the same time. He is going in the opposite direction, which means you have to make a U-turn. That 180-degree change in direction towards God is called "repentance."

Finally, there has to be a **clear view of Jesus**. You cannot follow Jesus if you can't see him clearly enough to follow him. He has to stay up front, visible, and leading the way in a clear path to follow.

A clear view of Jesus is what this book is all about. Thankfully and quite intentionally, we have the four Gospels of Matthew, Mark, Luke, and John in the New Testament that give us that clear view of Jesus. From those eyewitness accounts, I believe we can drill down to focus on seven major essentials in the life of Jesus. And it's those same essentials that we need today if we want to follow him.

It's time to get started. The Rabbi is calling.

The Way of Jesus
Questions for the Journey

Chapter One "Follow Me"

Before reading this chapter, how did you define what it meant to be a "Christian?"

Describe the difference between "Churchianity" and Christianity.

What was the one phrase that Jesus repeatedly used to call disciples?

In order to know and follow Jesus we have to change in three ways:

1.) Change in our (Direction)

2.) Change in our (Beliefs)

3.) Change in our (Purpose)

How are you seeing these changes happen in your life?

What are some of the challenges you currently face in making these changes?

What do you need to do today in order to begin or continue the journey of following Jesus?

Chapter Two
The Way of Jesus and the Father

And a voice came from heaven, "You are my beloved Son, with you I am well pleased." (Mark 1:11)

As the ancient Chinese proverb says, "A journey of a thousand miles begins with a single step."

The first step in this journey of following Jesus to become more like him is to first understand and learn from the relationship that Jesus had with God the Father. As we will see, it was a relationship built on intimacy and dependency. Nothing was more essential to the life of Jesus than this relationship. Everything that Jesus said and did was a direct result of what he first enjoyed and cultivated with the Father.

The Bible doesn't tell us exactly when or how Jesus came to an awakening in this relationship. But, in the second chapter of Luke, we are given a rare glimpse into Jesus' boyhood years when, at the age of twelve, as the family was visiting Jerusalem, Jesus was accidentally left behind by his parents.

Imagine that conversation.

"Do you have Jesus?"

"No, I thought you had him."

"Well, I thought you had him."

"Great, we've just lost the Son of God and Savior of the world."

(To all the parents out there, be encouraged. Even Mary and Joseph didn't get it right all the time.)

When they finally found Jesus three days later, he was in the temple, listening to and grilling the religious leaders of his day. In response to Mary and Joseph's exasperation that I imagine went something like "What on earth were you thinking?"

Jesus showed he clearly understood his calling early on when in Luke 2:49 (NIV) he said: *"Did you not know I must be about my Father's business?"*

Silence. (Twelve-year-old kids are so much fun, aren't they?)

Even at twelve years of age, Jesus claimed he had a special relationship with God the Father (a claim that no one else in his day would have ever been bold enough to make for fear of being labeled a heretic or insane.)

It was a relationship that only grew and deepened with time. By my count, there are forty-one times in the Gospels where Jesus used the term "My Father" in reference to God. As we see in Scripture, this intimate relationship with the Father was essential to how Jesus lived his life.

So, what did that look like and how do we apply it to our lives today? Let's take a look.

Loving the Father

On one occasion, Jesus was asked the question, "What is the first or most important commandment of them all?"

Jesus answered him:

"The first of all the commandments is: Hear O Israel, the Lord our God, the Lord is one, and you shall love the Lord your God with all your heart, with all your soul, and with all your mind, and with all your strength. This is the first commandment."
(Mark 12:29-30 MEV)

Jesus went on to say that the second greatest commandment is to love your neighbor as you would love yourself. Apparently, for Jesus, when you love God as Scripture commands you to do, you will also love those around you.

Again, Jesus reduced all of the laws of Judaism down to just two, two simple and beautiful commands.

Jesus' love for the Father came first, before anything or anyone else. In turn, that love for the Father determined the entire direction and purpose of Jesus' life. We tend to make the life and ministry of Jesus, including the cross, all about his love for *us*, which in turn makes it all about *us*. Sorry to burst your bubble, but it is not all about us. We are not the center of the universe. For Jesus, it was all about his love for the Father—with all of his heart, soul, mind, and strength. Love for us was certainly there, but further down the list.

In the same way, following Jesus for us today must also begin with our love for God. It is not a religious thing; it's a relational thing. It is not about "living a good life;" it's about loving the one *who is life.*

Dear reader, please remember that loving God is more than just words. Like the old adage goes, "Love is a verb." Love for the Father is living a life that is totally focused on the object of that love while, at the same time, putting that love into practice.

Jesus said it best in John 14:31 (MEV): *"But I do as the Father has commanded me, so that the world may know that I love the Father."*

I'm afraid that because love has been so postured and pimped by our culture today, we have become blind to the fact that love is something we *give.* Love is selfless, not selfish. It's not primarily concerned with its own needs and desires, but those of others.

Jesus so loved the Father, and you and me, that he gave everything, even his life. That is real love.

I recently shared a few words at a funeral service for a twenty-nine-year-old woman who had been completely disabled from birth. Jessica was completely dependent on her parents for everything, and for twenty-nine years that is exactly what her parents gave her—everything. Jessica's parents had organized their entire lives around caring for their daughter. On the day we gathered to celebrate Jessica's life, I told the family that their lives and their love for their daughter would forever be a beautiful picture of what real love looks like. Because love is a verb.

Knowing the Father

Jesus loved the Father because he intimately *knew* the Father. In the same way, if we want to grow in a love relationship with our heavenly Father, we have to begin with getting to know him.

Jesus was the world's greatest theologian. Consider that theology, in the simplest of terms, is the study of God. Theology was once considered the queen of sciences. And why not? What could be more important than knowing more about the one who created us?

Loving God requires us to be theologians as well. The better we know him, the more we will love him. The bigger and greater God is to us, the bigger and greater our love will be for him. Our love for God becomes anemic when our knowledge of God becomes anemic.

One of the leading voices today challenging believers to a more passionate love relationship with God is renowned pastor and theologian, John Piper. In his epic book, *Desiring God*, Piper calls us to a hedonistic lifestyle of enjoying God—one that is unabashed in our pursuit of him as we grow more in love with him every day. The only way we can truly enjoy God is by knowing him.

As we learn of him in Scripture.

As we sit in holy silence.

As we hear him in the laughter of children.

As we catch subtle glimpses of him in the beauty of a flower.

As we stand awestruck of him at a sunset.

As we feel our smallness by the vastness of the universe. He's all around us.

My encouragement to you, dear reader, is to spend the rest of your life getting to know the Father. Only then will you be able to truly love him and follow in the way of Jesus.

Time with the Father

One of the major themes in the Gospel of Luke is the prayer life of Jesus.

"In these days he went out to the mountain to pray and all night he continued in prayer to God." (Luke 6:12)

I have to admit, I have never climbed a mountain to spend the night in prayer. I've never even considered it. You probably haven't either. (If you have, high fives and way to go!) Most of us prefer the comfort of our bed and a night of sleep to hours of prayer, but not Jesus. He prioritized time alone with the Father above all else. He prayed in every situation. Before every major decision, Jesus prayed. Then again, after long periods of ministry, Jesus sought out the Father in prayer.

Yet, no one has ever had a closer relationship with the Father than Jesus. In John 10:30, Jesus even said, *"I and the Father are one."*

If prayer was vital to the life of Jesus, who was "one with the Father," how much more should we value the necessity of staying connected to God through prayer in our own lives today?

Remember how it felt the last time you lost your phone? See, just the thought of being disconnected from our devices sends us into a panic. If only we understood that prayer is our direct connection to the Father and guarded that line of communication like we do our smart phones. Prayer allows us to be in intimate conversation with the Father—an unfiltered conversation where we can share our hurts, our fears, our dreams, our very hearts, and where he will speak back. It's just a matter of listening.

When you think of prayer, what comes to mind? Maybe it sounds something like, "Oh, Thou, who sits upon the throne of highest heaven as the Holy of Holies and Ancient of Days." That could be the language you use when you pray or have heard when others pray, but it doesn't have to be. Some of the most powerful prayers in the Bible were just a few, simple words: "God, be merciful to me a sinner." Or, like the prayer of the thief hanging on the cross next to Jesus: "Jesus, remember me when you come into your kingdom."

Short. Simple. Powerful.

The most beautiful prayers I have ever heard actually came from children. Recently, our two-year-old grand-daughter, Nora, looked up and prayed, "Yeshua, I love you. And my neck hurts." A simple prayer of worship and dependency. Maybe that's why Jesus told us we need to become like children in order to enter into the kingdom of God.

Authentic prayer comes in different forms. Sometimes it is lofty and eloquent; other times it is simple and child-like. It may be tears and sobs at times, and sometimes, there may not be any words at all. Prayer can also be just listening—yes, just listening in silence for the still, small voice of God who whispers to your heart.

If you have never tried that, why not here and now? Try it, come on, you can do this. Put the book down and take some time to *just listen.*

As a "papa," one of the things that makes me smile is to whisper things into my grandchildren's ear. Usually it's something like "Papa loves you very much." Just about every time I give those whispers, that little one will get really still and truly listen to what I am saying. What makes me smile most is when they lean in a second or third time and ask me to say it again. (I'm smiling right now as I write this.)

Little one, I hope that you are making time each day to "lean in" and listen to what the Father is trying to whisper to your heart. What Jesus teaches us is that when we love the Father as he did, we will spend time with the Father as he did. Only then are we ready to take the next step.

Depending on the Father

Jesus never did anything apart from the Father. Let's take a look at what he said in the Gospel of John:

"So Jesus said to them, 'truly, truly, I say to you, the Son can do nothing of his own accord, but only what he sees the Father

doing. For whatever the Father does, that the Son does likewise.'"
(John 5:19)

"For I have not spoken on my own authority, but the Father who sent me has himself given me a commandment—what to say and what to speak." (John 12:49)

Every word Jesus spoke and every step he took was prompted and directed by the Father. From start to finish, Jesus lived a life completely dependent on the Father's guidance. His teaching. His miracles. His power. His compassion. Dare I say it … even his suffering. It all came from the Father as Jesus lived a life of depending on the dependability of the Father.

Here is the really amazing part. (I hope I'm about to blow your mind here.)

In John 14:12, Jesus said:

"Truly, truly, I say to you, whoever believes in me will also do the works that I do; and greater works than these will he do, because I am going to the Father."

Whoa, did you get that? Did you catch the word "greater?" Yes, that's what Jesus said—that we would do greater works than he did. Let that sink in for a moment. You are probably thinking, how is that possible? I mean, we are talking heavy-duty miracles here: feeding hungry multitudes of people with just one kid's sack lunch, healing the sick, raising the dead. How could we do greater works than that?

It is entirely possible and even to be expected because we serve the same Father that Jesus served. God has not changed. He is the same yesterday, today, and forever. And in a world of constant and accelerating change, that's reassuring to know, isn't it?

So, if the Father hasn't changed, it stands to reason that we should never be surprised by miracles today. But that can only genuinely happen as we depend on the Father just as Jesus did.

For those of us who live in Western culture, that is easier said than done. We have been blessed with so much in terms of material things. In comparison to the rest of the world, the West is rich ... and getting richer. What is meant to be a blessing, can also become a curse. In material and physical terms, we sometimes think that we do not need God. *We are doing pretty well all by ourselves, thank you very much.* Here in the Western world, learning to truly depend on God is an uphill climb for most of us. So, how do we cultivate a life of total dependence on the Father?

A good start would be to consider taking some "exits" off of the cozy, comfortable, and safe route of Easy Street. In other words, find an exit out of your comfort zone. It might be serving at a soup kitchen or shelter in your community. It might be a short-term or long-term mission trip with a local church that is more than just "volun-tourism" or a "mission-cation"—a mission trip that is truly to help the impoverished and lost, not one used as a good excuse to travel the world. It might be mentoring at-risk youth. It might be adoption or foster care. The opportunities are all around us. We just have to be willing to open our eyes and take the road less paved with the comforts we've become so accustomed to in our prosperous society—a path that requires us to be completely dependent on the Father.

Obeying the Father

Another key to a growing relationship with the Father that we learn from the life of Jesus is his complete obedience to the will of the Father. There are so many examples but let's take a look at just a few:

"For I have come down from heaven, not to do my own will, but the will of him who sent me." (John 6:38)

"Jesus said to them, my food is to do the will of him who sent me and to accomplish his work." (John 4:34)

"And he withdrew from them about a stone's throw, and knelt down and prayed, saying 'Father, if you are willing, remove this cup from me. Nevertheless, not my will, but yours, be done.'" (Luke 22:41-42)

At every turn and in every decision, Jesus had a passion to obey the will of the Father. It's the very thing he came to earth to accomplish. Jesus even referred to the will of the Father as his "food." Doing the will of the Father was his "steak and potatoes." It was essential to his life.

All of the miracles, all who were healed, all who were

fed, all who were touched and blessed by Jesus, were all the will of the Father. And what that tells us is that the will of the Father is *always good.*

Sometimes we have this idea that following God's will is going to deprive us of something. We have this idea that God is a cosmic killjoy character that frowns on anything that we perceive as fun or enjoyable or good. That is just not true. Everything that Jesus did was the will of the Father, and it was all good. Jesus turned water into wine at a wedding (a *lot* of wine). And it wasn't just average wine, it was the best of wine. That doesn't sound like a killjoy to me. Do not believe the lies of the enemy. The will of God for your life is good. In fact, it is very good. Because God is good.

How did Jesus know the will of the Father? We already know that Jesus prayed, and he prayed often. Prayer is definitely a key to knowing God's will. Even more than prayer, knowing the will of God is in knowing the Word of God. Jesus knew the will of the Father because he knew the Word of the Father.

When Jesus was tempted, how did he respond? It was with Scripture. When Jesus taught, he taught from the Scriptures. When Jesus had to respond to the attacks of the religious leaders, he responded with Scripture. Even while dying on the cross, Jesus quoted the Scriptures.

This is the secret for knowing God's will for your life. If you want to know his will, then you have to know his Word.

And of course, because Jesus knew the Scriptures, he

knew the will of the Father would take him to the cross. The cross was the pinnacle of obedience for Jesus. It was the culmination of all that preceded it, when Jesus could look at his rendezvous with suffering and sin on the cross and say, "Bring it on."

In the blockbuster movie *The Matrix*, there is a scene when Neo is face to face with the dreaded and deadly Smith. Neo could either turn and run or stay and fight. The safe thing to do would be to turn and run, but instead, he decides to stay and fight. With a simple gesture of his hand, Neo invites Smith to "bring it on."

It was Jesus, our real-life Neo, who in fact did give his life to win the battle between good and evil. It was Jesus who was completely, even in the face of death, obedient to the will of the Father. It was Jesus who in reality faced all that evil could throw at him and by doing so basically said, "Bring it on."

It is not surprising then to discover that Jesus calls us into that same life of obedience. In fact, you cannot follow Jesus without it. To somehow think we can follow Jesus without obeying Jesus is what my good friend Jim Dennis calls "broken thinking." That kind of thinking is a contradiction to what Jesus himself teaches us.

> *"If you love me, you will keep my commandments."*
> *(John 14:15)*

It's difficult to argue with that. If you do, it is an argument you will lose every time. Clearly, to follow Jesus requires obedience to him. That does not mean that we do it perfectly. However, it does mean that, like Neo in *The Matrix*, we don't turn to run from the battle, but rather we stand and fight.

Eugene Peterson's title to his wonderful little book captures the essence of what a life of obedience to God looks like: *A Long Obedience in the Same Direction*. And that direction is covered in the dust of Jesus.

The Way of Jesus
Questions for the Journey

Chapter Two "Jesus and The Father"

According to Mark 12:28-34, what did Jesus value above all other things?

How did Jesus model what love for God looks like?

How would you describe your love for God at this point in your life?

What stands in your way of loving God more? What is competing for that love?

Imagine loving God as Jesus loved him. What would that look like in practical ways for you?

Chapter Three
The Way of Jesus and Community

And let us consider how to stir up one another to love and good works, not neglecting to meet together, as is the habit of some, but encouraging one another, and all the more as you see the Day drawing near. (Hebrews 10:24-25)

Community was another essential in the life of Jesus. When Jesus began his ministry, one of the first things he did was to identify and call a group of men to come and do life alongside him. The Gospel of Mark gives us some insight into what that process looked like:

"And he went up on the mountain and called to him those whom he desired, and they came to him. And he appointed twelve (whom he also named apostles) so that they might be with him and he might send them out to preach and have authority to cast out demons."
(Mark 3:13-15)

From that time forward, the apostles—this band of brothers—were right beside Jesus, following him and learning from him in an adventure of a lifetime. They would never again be the same.

What does this teach us about community? What is

community and what does it look like? What is the purpose of being in community?

First, the Gospels tell us that Jesus *valued* community. Luke's Gospel adds something interesting to this same account from Mark. According to Luke, Jesus spent the entire night on the mountain in prayer prior to choosing his disciples. That alone tells us that this was a decision Jesus did not take lightly. He prayed it through first. This was important. This community of brothers mattered.

From Mark 3:14, we could even say that Jesus *needed* community. Notice the verse says that Jesus called them so that "they might be with him." One way to interpret that verse is to assume it is talking about how these men needed to be with Jesus. That is certainly true. They needed to be with Jesus and learn from him through his teaching and example. Another way of looking at this verse is to understand that Jesus needed them as well. Jesus needed community.

How could Jesus "need" community? How could God himself need anything? Welcome to the mystery of the incarnation. It is the mystery of God who became one of us. The way Jesus needed community was the same way he needed food. It was the same way he needed water and needed sleep and needed time alone to pray and worship. This is the mystery of God becoming flesh and blood.

As Eugene Peterson famously says in The Message version of John 1:14, *"The Word became flesh and blood, and moved into the neighborhood."* When Jesus "moved into our neighborhood," he became just like us.

My point here is that if Jesus needed community, then stop and consider how much more we need community today. We cannot do life on our own.

As the English poet John Donne wrote, "No man is an island." You may want to visit or even live on an island with beautiful white beaches and crystal-clear waters, but you were not created to live isolated and insulated from the rest of the world. You and I were never meant to do life alone. Whether you like it or not, you need me, and I need you.

Science is only now discovering what Jesus was trying to teach us. According to a seventy-five-year Harvard study of 724 men, both from Harvard and from inner-city Boston, we need relationships to thrive. The study found that men who had close family and friend relationships were happier and even healthier. Little wonder then that the Bible is full of encouragement for us to do life together.

"But, Mike, that church is just a bunch of hypocrites." Yeah, I can't tell you how many times I've heard that one. But just stop and think about the kind of guys Jesus called to be his twelve apostles. They were smelly fishermen, a tax collector, a political zealot, slow to understand and even believe, one denied knowing Jesus, and another helped himself to the money bag and then betrayed Jesus to the authorities. Yet, these were the guys who Jesus handpicked to be his closest friends. Wow, that church down the road might not be so bad after all.

No matter how imperfect and broken your local fellowship of believers might be, you still need them, and they still need you. Just like Jesus, we all need community.

A Picture of Community

In calling and training these twelve men as apostles, Jesus gives us a picture of what an effective, transformational community looks like.

One of the first observations is the size of this community. Jesus chose a smaller group of only twelve men. Most of you who are reading this right now probably have been to or are currently attending a larger faith community that we typically refer to as a "church." Just remember that the church is not a building, but rather the people who meet in that building or home.

Although most churches today consist of less than a hundred members, the megachurch model made up of thousands of people who attend and serve in that context has become popular in our society. Regardless of whether your larger community is one hundred or one thousand, that larger faith community is not really conducive to real life change and transformation.

Don't get me wrong, I am not slamming church. I am *for* the church, and I serve the church. However, a typical Sunday morning experience at a typical Sunday morning church may be great for worship, fellowship, and encouragement from the Bible, but not so much for discipleship. That is exactly why someone can be a good church member for decades but never really become more like Jesus.

Remember my definition of a disciple? It is someone who is following Jesus to become more like him. But so many of our churches are filled with people who are less like Jesus than many of those outside the church. Can you think of someone like that right now? Yeah, I thought you could.

Real life change that makes us more like Jesus happens in smaller environments. This is why Jesus spent most of his time with the twelve disciples instead of with the large crowds who followed him.

Not only that, we see in Scripture that Jesus spent additional time with an inner circle composed of Peter, James, and John.

It doesn't matter whether your circle is three or twelve. There's no magic number that makes up a Jesus-focused community. The point is that your circle needs to be small enough to be able to build healthy relationships and hold each other accountable to grow in your faith.

There is also the element of time to consider. Jesus spent a lot of time with the twelve. In fact, it was pretty much 24/7 for three solid years. It doesn't appear that Jesus took many breaks from his community other than for prayer and solitude. They went everywhere Jesus went so that they were a part of everything he did.

Jesus fed 5,000 people, and they were there.

Jesus calmed the storm on the Sea of Galilee, and they were there—afraid, wet, and probably a little seasick.

Jesus cast out a legion of demons from a man, and they were there—wide-eyed and afraid.

Jesus raised Lazarus from the dead, and they were there.

Jesus healed the sick, and they were there.

Jesus was arrested in the garden, and they were there.

Jesus was nailed to a cross, and they were … well, hiding. (They still had a long way to go.)

I hope you get the picture here.

Real community that changes and transforms us is something that takes time. That's another weakness of Sunday morning "Churchianity." Imagine what would happen to your physical health if you only ate food once a week. You would be pretty weak and malnourished, right?

It works the same way with our spiritual health. Yet, so many people think that attending a church service once or twice a week is all they need to become more like Jesus. That's not at all what we see of Jesus and his band of brothers, and that's not what we see reflected in the early Church. In the Book of Acts, the Bible tells us:

"They worshiped together at the Temple each day, met in homes for the Lord's Supper, and shared their meals with great joy and generosity." (Acts 2:46 NLT)

That doesn't sound much like Sunday-only "Churchianity," does it? Clearly, the early Church was committed to living together in community, and that community takes time to cultivate. But that seems to be the biggest hindrance we face to building community today. We have filled our days with so much coming and going and left little time for the one thing that Jesus called us to do—be discipled and make disciples.

So, how can we make more time for community with our already busy and over-booked schedules? Let me suggest a four-step process as a good place to start:

- Slow down. *The speed of light does not have to be your speed of life.*
- Determine your priorities. *Is being a disciple of Jesus important to you?*
- Practice subtraction rather than addition. *What can you remove from your calendar?*
- Repurpose how you are currently spending your time. *Use mealtime or gym time for community time.*

No matter how busy we are, making more time for community and discipleship can be done. It just takes some effort and discipline to make it happen. It must become a priority in our lives.

The Priority of Community

Community must be a priority, not an afterthought. We see this throughout the New Testament in the life of Jesus and the early Church. In just about every chapter of every book, the drumbeat of community can be heard. Over and over again we see the phrase "one another."

"Honor one another."

"Live in harmony with one another."

"Welcome one another."

"Greet one another with a holy kiss."

"Comfort one another."

"Bear one another's burdens."

"Encourage one another."

There are so many more, but I think you get the idea. Then, to top it all off, Jesus said in the Book of John:

> *"By this all people will know that you are my disciples, if you have love for one another." (John 13:35 MEV)*

What strikes me about this verse is that Jesus could have given any number of markers to indicate a disciple—theology, worship, rules and regulations, biblical knowledge, social justice, or _____ (You fill in the blank.). Jesus instead chose the marker of having love for one another. I hope that grabs you like it grabs me.

But guess what? The "one anothers" can only be lived out in a community with other believers. Not alone, and not even in a Sunday morning church setting where it's easy to slip in and slip out unseen and unchanged. You can't grow daily as a disciple apart from community. We were not created to do life alone. We need each other.

The Purpose of Community

Not only do we need community to be able to grow in our faith, we need community to fulfill our purpose.

The purpose of Jesus choosing the twelve is captured in a single word found in Mark 3:14-15—sent. Jesus *"sent them out to preach and to have authority to cast out demons."*

The word "apostle," a word that only now is being reclaimed by the Church after centuries of neglect and confusion, simply means "one who is sent." The apostles were not super saints or supermen or super anything. They were simply sent out to preach and to heal and to deliver with the very same authority as Jesus.

And because they obeyed the call to go, the Church was birthed, and you and I are here today.

Here is the beauty of authentic Jesus-led communities who follow the call to "go." Those who are serious about following Jesus are never content just to meet, eat and drink, maybe pray, maybe read the Word, only to check their religious boxes off for that week. Enough of that already. Jesus himself calls us into community for the purpose of invading—yes, invading—and then impacting a lost world with the gospel of his kingdom. In that sense, we are as much apostles as the original twelve. We are now the "sent ones." Sent out to preach, heal, and deliver.

Now, what that looks like really depends on the needs you see around you. (And I hope you see them.) Regardless of your local context, a sent community of "Jesus wannabes" must give itself to three things:

First, **share the gospel.** The gospel is the good news of Jesus' life, death, burial, and resurrection that rescues and redeems when received by faith. It is the good news that Jesus took my sins and your sins and became that sin for us on the cross, all so that through faith and repentance we could be saved from eternal death and hell.

And let me be clear … it is never enough just to *be* the good news. As good and as helpful as that certainly is, it must also include sharing the gospel so that others have an opportunity to hear it and respond in faith.

As a community, find ways that will give you the opportunity to tell others about Jesus. A great resource to help you do that is found in *The Gospel Primer* written by Caesar Kalinowski and available at www.missiopublishing.com. Read it, and then share it with your community as a way to become fluent in sharing the gospel.

Second, **meet the needs around you.** Everywhere Jesus went, he gave himself to meeting the physical, emotional, and spiritual needs of those around him.

Remember how Jesus turned that water into wine? (My Baptist denomination still struggles with that one.)

A multitude of hungry people needed food, and with the help of a boy's sack lunch of bread and fish, Jesus fed well over 5,000 people.

A man who was blind from birth needed his eyesight, and Jesus healed him on the spot. (Imagine Jesus being the first person you ever laid your eyes on!)

Two sisters named Mary and Martha needed Jesus to comfort them after the death of their brother Lazarus, and Jesus comforted them by raising Lazarus from the dead after four days.

The Gospels are full of ways that Jesus met the needs of

those around him. And as followers of Jesus, we are called to do the very same thing.

If you need a little convincing, just consider what Jesus said in "The Parable of the Sheep and Goats" in Matthew 25:33-46. In this story, Jesus talks about how, at his second coming, he will separate his true followers from those who are not, comparing it to separating the sheep from the goats.

Do you remember what the distinction was between the two? It was not in their faith, their knowledge, or their traditions. The real distinction was found in the response of his true followers to the needs of the hungry, the thirsty, the stranger, the naked, and the prisoner.

Those same needs are all around us today. Yes, right where you live, and maybe even right next door. Just look around you and then get busy.

Third, **push back the darkness.** Mark 3:15 tells us that Jesus gave the apostles the authority to "cast out demons." Okay, I know this topic makes many believers uncomfortable. In our Western culture this sounds strange, and we would rather not talk about the devil and his demons. But how else can we explain evil? How else can we explain things like human trafficking, the drug trade, the murder rate in Chicago, or the horrors of Auschwitz or Aleppo? Or, how do we explain the mass shootings in places like Las Vegas or Sutherland Springs? Is it just human nature gone bad, or is it something more?

Jesus knew that it was more than just broken humanity, and a large part of his ministry was devoted to exposing

51

and pushing back the darkness of evil and the spiritual forces that represent that evil.

One beautiful example is found in Mark 5:1-20 when Jesus and the apostles encounter a man who was possessed by demons. Since we do not know this man's name, we refer to him as "Legion" because he was possessed by a legion of demons. (A Roman legion was a military unit made up of sometimes more than 7,000 soldiers.) The man was naked and living among the tombs, dangerous to himself and anyone around him. Legion is a gruesome and disturbing picture of what evil can do to a person. He had lost everything, even his real name.

In this account, Jesus quickly and firmly cast out the legion of demons and sent them into a herd of pigs nearby, leaving this man, whose life had been so broken and scarred by evil, completely free and healed.

It was just another day in the life and ministry of Jesus and the twelve.

Clearly, if we have a hard time believing in demons, we will have a hard time following in the way of Jesus. The greatest purpose of a Jesus-led community is to push back the darkness and expose that darkness for what it really is—the work of an enemy who hates God and who hates us.

When we were serving as missionaries in Costa Rica, the town where we lived was considered a "party town" and known for drugs and prostitution. Any time we took a walk through the town, we were approached by several people asking if we needed one or the other. It would have been easy to ignore or just avoid that kind of darkness.

But what do you think Jesus would have done? I think you know the answer.

So, our community started an outreach ministry called "The Light of Tamarindo." One night each month we would meet on the streets to pray, then go out and invite people to join us for a meal and share the gospel with those who would listen. Our conviction became that, instead of cursing and avoiding the darkness, Jesus has given us the authority to do something about it.

What does the darkness look like where you live? It might try to disguise itself as something less than what it is, but it's there. You can find it if you look, or it might find you. Don't be afraid of the darkness; just be the light. When you are the light, the darkness doesn't stand a chance. Jesus said so.

You may be wondering where to start in finding the kind of community I am describing here—the kind of community that we see in the life of Jesus and his disciples. My first response would be that such a community probably already exists where you live, but you may have to look around to find it. But, if after looking and asking around with no success, why not start your own community of faith? You don't have to be a pastor or missionary to do what Jesus did. Simply find some close friends who are spiritually hungry like you are and start learning to live like Jesus. Spend time reading and praying through the Gospels, and then just do what Jesus did.

This isn't rocket science. You can do this. You were made for this.

The Way of Jesus
Questions for the Journey

Chapter Three "Jesus and Community"

How important was it for Jesus to be in community?

Describe the kind of community that Jesus created around him.

According to John 13:35 what is the marker of being a disciple of Jesus? How does that require community?

Read Mark 3:13-15. What did Jesus create his community of disciples to do?

Describe your experience with this type of community.

What excuses stand in your way of finding a genuine community of believers?

Chapter Four
The Way of Jesus and the Kingdom

But seek first the kingdom of God and his righteousness, and all these things will be added to you. (Matthew 6:33)

How should following Jesus change the way that we live? I don't mean just on Sundays. How does it change our life at home, at school, at work, and when we're alone and no one is looking? If Jesus is our measure and model for what life should look like, then we cannot live a "business as usual" kind of life. Far from it.

When reading the Gospel accounts, we find that Jesus had much to say about life in the "kingdom of God." In fact, when I started counting the references, the Gospels use that phrase some fifty-four times. Then, in Matthew's Gospel, the alternative phrase "kingdom of heaven" is used thirty-one times. One doesn't use a term that often without reason. It must have significant meaning.

In the Book of Mark, we see that this was Jesus' main message from the beginning of his ministry:

"Now after John was put in prison, Jesus came to Galilee, preaching the gospel of the kingdom of God, and saying, 'The time is fulfilled, and the kingdom of God is at hand. Repent, and believe in the gospel.'" (Mark 1:14-15 MEV)

57

Before looking at the big picture of life in the kingdom, there are a couple of things that beg for our attention in these two verses.

First, Jesus was a preacher. *"Jesus came to Galilee, preaching."*

Don't miss that. Don't let that go unnoticed. Because, in our Western culture today, preachers are usually stereotyped and caricatured as intolerant, hypocritical, loud, and sometimes even shady. Preachers are right down there with … well, you fill in the blank. We don't see many positive portrayals of ministers and preachers. Some of it is deserved, but much of it is not.

But Jesus first came "preaching." If this is your tribe, if this is your calling, if this is your passion and ministry—be encouraged. Don't listen to the voices and images of our culture that mock and ridicule what you do. Know that you are in good company. You are following in the steps of Jesus. When the going gets tough, and it will, and you are thinking about calling it quits, just remember Jesus. Keep your eyes on Jesus. Follow his example. Preach.

Maybe you are not in vocational ministry. Maybe you teach school or repair cars or prepare taxes. Know that you are still called to preach. In fact, you are already preaching. The way you live your life is a sermon that those around you are listening to and learning from. What are you preaching? I hope that your life is a sermon that is pointing others to Jesus.

Second, right from the beginning of his ministry, Jesus was preaching the gospel or what is also called the "good news" of the kingdom of God. This was the main thing for Jesus. And, as I have already pointed out, Jesus had a lot to say to us and show us about the kingdom.

Sometimes he used parables or stories to help us understand more about his kingdom. Perhaps Jesus' most famous teaching on the kingdom is what we refer to as "The Sermon on the Mount."

If you haven't read the "Sermon on the Mount" or if it has been a while, why not put down this book and grab a Bible? Turn to the Book of Matthew and read chapters five through seven. Read the whole thing. And don't just read it, absorb it. Let it soak into your soul and ponder the kind of life that Jesus is describing. Go ahead; it's just three chapters.

Back again? Good. That was pretty radical stuff, right? Did you catch the part about loving your enemies or the part about turning the other cheek? How about if your hand causes you to sin, cut it off?

There is no doubt that life in the kingdom is a radically different life. This was the core of everything Jesus was teaching us and showing us. For Jesus, the kingdom was a big deal. And if it was that important to Jesus, it should be even more important to us – which is exactly why I have included this chapter on life in the kingdom as an essential part of following Jesus.

A third thing to notice here is that the kingdom was "at hand." In other words, the kingdom of God was not a future hope but a present reality. Yes, there is more of the kingdom still to come, which is why Jesus taught us to pray,

"Thy kingdom come, thy will be done on earth as it is in heaven," but for Jesus the kingdom was here and now. The wait was over. The promise was fulfilled. The darkness was fading.

Because here is the amazing truth that I want you to see—Jesus *is* the kingdom. The kingdom was "at hand" because Jesus was at hand. The reign and rule of Jesus is the kingdom. Wherever you find Jesus as king, you find the kingdom.

Dear reader, you don't have to wait and hope for God's kingdom to come in some distant future. It's already here. If you follow and love Jesus, then you are a part of that kingdom. We don't see it or experience it perfectly because we are not perfect. Since we are broken, the kingdom that we see and experience appears to be broken at times. That is why your church has so many rough edges and you've been tempted to walk away. That is why followers of Jesus don't always look very much like Jesus. Since we are broken, the kingdom of God will look broken to us. But, make no mistake, the kingdom is here. Every believer is a representative of that kingdom. Every church that preaches the gospel is an embassy of that kingdom and a small glimmer of hope at what is to come when one day the kingdom will change everything.

A final thing I want you to notice is that Jesus called for a response to the kingdom. It was simply to "repent and believe the gospel."

In case you have not heard the word "repent" in a while, it means to turn away from sin and self. It's not just being sorry for something. You can be sorry for something you have done, but to truly repent, you have to turn away from it. I can be sorry for eating an entire container of chocolate ice cream, but that won't stop me from doing it again. But, if I repent, then I am going to stop buying the chocolate ice cream. (Yes, I love chocolate ice cream, by the way.) That is repentance, and until we truly repent and turn away from sin and self, we can't really take the next step.

After repentance, Jesus preached that we were to believe in the gospel or the "good news" of the kingdom. There are those today who are preaching a gospel of "it doesn't matter what you believe as long as you believe something." Well, that may sound nice and politically correct, but it is not what Jesus was preaching. His message was always to believe the gospel of the kingdom—a kingdom with Jesus as its king.

When we begin to really dig down deep to what Jesus said and showed us about the kingdom of God, what do we see? What picture emerges? Let me give it to you in a way that, for me, is easy to remember. Kingdom living is different living. In fact, it's radically different living. Let's take a look at this difference in Jesus' life.

His Values were Different.

Clearly, Jesus had a radically different value system compared to the culture around him. I have heard it said that Jesus was counter-cultural, but I believe Jesus went way beyond that. It could be said that Jesus was extra-cultural, in that he lived life on a different plane or different level. Yes, Jesus was a product of his culture and reflected that culture, just like you and I reflect our culture, but his values were different.

First, **Jesus valued people over things.** In fact, Jesus never had any of the material things that we today might consider essential or at least important. He owned no house or car. He had no bank account or retirement. It seems that the only material things that Jesus owned were the clothes on his back and, at his crucifixion, even those were taken from him.

Isn't it amazing that the One who could have had anything, chose to have nothing?

It's evident in Scripture that Jesus cared about people above possessions:

That's why he fed the hungry.

That's why he healed the sick (sometimes without even being asked).

That's why he wept at Lazarus's tomb (right before he raised him from the dead).

That's why he engaged in conversation with a Samaritan woman, breaking all kinds of cultural rules in the process.

That's why he was labeled "friend of sinners." He valued *all* people from *every* walk of life.

So how does this translate into the life of a follower of Jesus today? For starters, our priorities should look different from the rest of the world. The "American dream" and all the wealth and success that accompany it are not the highest pursuit in the life of a follower of Jesus. It's not that material things are bad; it's just that Jesus and his kingdom are better.

As John Piper has famously reminded us, "don't waste your life" chasing after things. Chase after Jesus. Pursue the people around you who need to experience the love and hope of Jesus.

Don't let it be said of us that which was said of the church of Laodicea in Revelation 3:17 (NKJV):

"Because you say, 'I am rich, have become wealthy, and have need of nothing'—and do not know that you are wretched, miserable, poor, blind, and naked."

These were strong words for this early church and it's a reminder for us today: Let us not be "rich" in things and poor in what matters most.

Second, **Jesus valued grace over the Law.** Again, when the woman caught in adultery was dragged before him by her accusers, she could have been stoned to death according to the Jewish law. The Law was pretty harsh about such things. Jesus chose grace over the Law. He chose not to condemn her with the Law but rather to redeem her with grace. *That* is the good news of the gospel. *That* is the kingdom.

The Law will always condemn us by showing us our sin. It judges our sin with stones and death, and that is its purpose. The Law drags us out into the street to be exposed for what we really are and for all of the shameful

63

things we have done.

But Jesus ushered in a new way—the way of grace. Instead of condemning our sin, he covers our sin with forgiveness. It was not that the Law was not important; it was. It was so important that Jesus kept the Law perfectly for us in order to fulfill its demands. Because he fulfilled the Law, Jesus could then replace the Law with grace.

For followers of Jesus today, there is no room for legalism. If we are saved by grace, and we are, then we must live by grace both to ourselves and to others. Live with the grace to love people just as they are and not as we wish they would be. Live with the grace to give God time to do what only he can do—change hearts. Live with the grace to break down every wall and barrier between the gospel and those who need it.

Thirdly, **Jesus valued obedience over comfort.** Again, Jesus obeyed the Law perfectly for us. He did for us what we could not do for ourselves. He lived in perfect obedience to the Word and the will of the Father, even when it was difficult. As a result, there was nothing comfortable about Jesus' life. On one occasion, Jesus told a would-be follower in Matthew 8:20, "Foxes have holes and birds of the air have nests, but the Son of Man has nowhere to lay his head." Jesus had nowhere to call home.

Think about that. The Creator, the One who created foxes to have holes and birds to have nests, chose to live without that same comfort of home. And it didn't stop there.

The One who never knew hunger became hungry.

The One who never grew tired had to sleep.

The One who never felt weakness became fatigued.

The One who never knew sin became sin for us.

All in perfect obedience to the Father. This was the life that Jesus lived, and it was not easy or comfortable—which means that choosing to follow Jesus will definitely take you out of your comfort zone.

In most of the world today, following Jesus is costly, even dangerous. Ask any believer in the Muslim world about how "comfortable" it is for them to follow Jesus. I know a pastor who lives in a part of the world where he can't find a job because he is a Christian. He tells me of attacks on Christians where many have died, and where some have even been burned alive because of their faith in Jesus. I heard from him just recently that his church had been bombed—again. It's not easy or comfortable or even safe for this pastor, but he has chosen obedience over comfort. He has chosen to live in the way of Jesus.

In light of such suffering, what right do we have to live in comfort? What right do we have in the Western world to live in luxury when the rest of our brothers and sisters live in poverty? Even in writing these words I am convicted.

You may be wondering where obedience to Jesus will take you. In my experience, it often takes you to dark places, poor places, and hard places where you wouldn't normally go. Don't ever confuse comfort with blessing. The true blessing comes with obedience—wherever that path may lead.

Fourth, **Jesus valued truth over success.** Jesus not

only spoke the truth; he *was* the truth. Sometimes telling the truth isn't the popular thing to do. There were times when Jesus said some hard things. Remember? It was that thing about hating your father and mother and that thing about drinking his blood and eating his flesh. It was that thing about taking up your cross and dying in order to follow him. Jesus never pulled his punches to speak the truth. As a result, soon after saying such things, the crowds that had been following Jesus slowly began looking for the exits.

They left. The truth was too difficult for them. *What is this guy talking about? This is crazy. I'm moving my membership. I didn't sign up for this.*

His following dwindled so much so that Jesus even turned to his own disciples and said, "Will you be leaving as well?"

Jesus went from "megachurch" status following down to almost no following with each difficult truth about the sacrifice that kingdom living required.

I don't know about you, but I doubt that Jesus would be invited to very many of our church growth conferences today. What breakout session would Jesus lead? I don't think he would be the headliner for the "Bigger, Faster, Stronger" church growth conference this year.

After all, what is success? What is success in life? In ministry? Is it more things, more people, more promotions, more influence? Not according to Jesus. He would have none of it. He avoided all the trappings of what we today would consider success in his life and ministry. We would do well to do the same. As many others have said before me, Jesus never calls us to be successful, only faithful. And the only way to be faithful is to know and to live the truth of God's Word.

His Purpose was Different.

Jesus was different in purpose, on purpose. First and foremost, that purpose was to glorify the Father rather than himself. This is the purpose of living in the kingdom of God. The kingdom is not here for me and you. The kingdom of God is all about the Father being glorified in all things. That is the ultimate reason why Jesus came to earth, suffered, died, and rose again. From start to finish, Jesus was all about the glory of God. Even when Jesus said that he came "to seek and to save that which was lost," it was all so that the Father would be glorified.

Yes, I am so very thankful that Jesus came to seek and to save you and me. Many years ago, at the age of seventeen, Jesus sought me and found me. But I am more thankful that Jesus came to glorify the Father. You see, we get it wrong when we say the gospel is all about us or that the kingdom is all about us or that the Bible is all about us. How is that different from any other "self-helpism" in the self-help section down at the local bookstore today? It's not. That is not the gospel. It's not about your glory, it's about God's glory.

Several years ago, Pastor Rick Warren published his bestseller *The Purpose Driven Life* and the first sentence on the first page of the book is: "It's not about you." And he is exactly right. It is not about you, and it's not about me. It is all about the glory of God.

That was Jesus' purpose. And that is our purpose.

His Teaching was Different.

Jesus was different in his teaching and preaching. Mark 1:22 (**NKJV**) tells us this:

"And they were astonished at his teaching for he taught them as one having authority, and not as the Scribes."

Apparently, this was the usual reaction to the teaching of Jesus—astonishment. All the other teachers of his day had to appeal to the authority of others. They had to rely on what others had said or written. So-and-so had to quote from so-and-so, but not Jesus. Jesus was different. He had a unique authority that allowed him to say things like, "You have heard it said, but I say to you."

And, the result was astonishment from many who heard him.

In other cases, it was anger. Whenever you read about the religious leaders interacting with Jesus, they were usually angry at something he said or did. He didn't play their game. He didn't tow the party line. He refused to budge one inch on the truth of God's Word or ways. Jesus was their conscience and their judge, and when they could listen no more, they decided he had to go.

That is life in the kingdom. Sometimes, you get to speak comfort and grace. You get to "comfort the afflicted." At other times, following Jesus will lead you to say the hard things to "afflict the comfortable." And, like Jesus, it will usually cost you something.

His Leadership was Different.

Someone once defined leadership as influence, and no one has influenced our world more than Jesus. What we need to see here is that, as a leader, Jesus was different. One reason we are still talking about Jesus today is because of that difference. Most leadership models that we now see (even in the church I'm afraid) are a "top-down" style of leadership. It's the model of leadership where the person at the top leads and directs the work of those below him or her in the organization, all so that those below can make the person at the top look really good. Of course, that helps to justify the salaries at the top.

What concerns me is the church has become so institutionalized that we have been forced to adopt this same model of leadership. We have borrowed our models from the world instead of the other way around. Pastors are now CEOs. Flow charts are required reading. Church has become "big business." The bottom line of a budget has become the bottom line for ministry. The staff meeting is now more important than the prayer meeting.

In contrast, Jesus modeled a "bottom-up" style of leadership.

In Matthew 20:28 (NKJV), Jesus said:

"The Son of Man did not come to be served, but to serve and to give His life a ransom for many."

What I don't want you to miss here is that Jesus had every right to be served. He was God in the flesh. He was the "chief executive" of all chief executives. Everyone should have been serving him. But in this great reversal of roles, Jesus came to serve. That word "serve" in the original language of the Bible literally means to serve others like a waiter or waitress would serve customers at a restaurant. The next time you eat at a restaurant and are served by a waiter or waitress, think of Jesus, picture Jesus as your waiter. That is the word he used. And then, in what surely must have been seared into the memory of the disciples, at the Passover meal right before the cross, Jesus became that servant and washed the feet of the disciples. Washing someone's feet was always welcomed and needed, but it was only done by servants and slaves. No one else would ever stoop so low (literally) to do such a thing. But Jesus did. He is our example of what real leadership looks like.

It's the leader who serves from the bottom up.

It's the leader who gives themselves away for the good of others and the glory of God.

It's the leader who takes the job no one else wants.

It's the leader who turns all the attention away from themselves to focus attention on others.

It's the leader who, instead of climbing up the ladder

of success, chooses to climb down that ladder.

It's the leader who looks like Jesus.

His Use of Power was Different.

Jesus was different in his use of power. Remember, Jesus was God, so he was all-powerful. At times, we are given glimpses of that power.

While crossing the Sea of Galilee, Jesus and the disciples were caught in a storm, and, with just a few words, Jesus calms the storm. One minute, the disciples are terrified at the storm, the next they are terrified of Jesus. Can you imagine them in that boat, soaking wet with fear, slowly backing away from Jesus and saying, "Who is this guy that even the wind and the waves obey his voice?"

It was not just the wind and waves that obeyed his voice. Demons obeyed his voice. Sickness obeyed his voice. The water that turned into wine obeyed his voice. The dead even obeyed his voice.

And, unlike how most earthly power is used, Jesus always used his power for good. So many times, power is abused and misused because it so often corrupts people. Just look at history. We even see this in the church. Just today, I heard the news of another respected and well-known pastor whose career is now over because of moral failure. It happens way too often. It's not because these are bad people, pretending to be something they are not. Like all the rest of us, these are broken people who cannot handle the power that comes with position and applause.

If you think you can handle it or that you can control it or that you can resist it on your own, then we need to talk. When you dance around the fire of applause and praise, you will get burned.

Unlike any person before or after him, Jesus knew how to handle power and he only used it to help, never to hurt. Nowhere in Scripture depicts this better than at the cross. Jesus had the power to avoid the cross. He had the power to turn a wooden cross into toothpicks. He had the power to vaporize those who drove the nails and who mocked him with words. But Jesus refused to go there.

"Father, forgive them for they know not what they do."

Remember that? That's a display of real power.

There were so many ways that Jesus was different in the way he lived his life. If we want to see what the kingdom of God is like, just look at Jesus. And if Jesus is our king, it's not a question of *if* our lives will be different, but to what degree our lives will be different. It's what being "salt and light" is all about.

Jesus said, *"You are the salt of the earth. You are the light of the world."* For Jesus, it was not a question of should be or could be, but rather "you are." That is what is going to happen if you follow Jesus. He will not lead you out of this world. But he will lead you to be different from this world.

A holy kind of different.

A kingdom-living kind of different.

A Jesus kind of different.

The Way of Jesus
Questions for the Journey

Chapter Four "Jesus and Life in the Kingdom"

Read Mark 1:14-15. What was Jesus preaching?

If Jesus is the Kingdom, what does it take to enter into that kingdom?

Are you in the kingdom of God? Is Jesus ruling your life?

If kingdom living is different living, how did Jesus model that for us?

If you are following Jesus, how is your life different now than it was before? What areas still need work?

Chapter Five
The Way of Jesus and Mission

As the Father has sent me, even so I am sending you. (John 20:21)

As I write these words today, I am sitting under a tree beside a soccer field in a little community called Pinilla, Costa Rica, and, in the heat of the day, I am very thankful for some shade. I am an outsider in this community. I look very different with my white skin and my greying—okay white—hair. I don't speak the language very well. At times, the culture seems strange and foreign to me. Even as I am writing this today a truck is passing by my shade tree with loudspeakers blaring "gallinas limpias" (clean hens) for sale. It's just another reminder that I'm not from here. We don't have trucks like that back in the states. I am simply a guest in a place far from home.

I wonder if that's how Jesus must have felt. Because, just as my wife and I feel called to missions here in Costa Rica, Jesus was called to missions as well. Jesus was a missionary. It's very clear from Scripture that Jesus understood that he had been sent by the Father on a mission.

In Luke 4:18 (NKJV), Jesus is in a synagogue and he stands to read the passage for that day. It's a reading from Isaiah:

"The Spirit of the Lord is upon Me, because He has anointed Me to preach the Gospel to the poor; He has sent me to heal the broken-hearted, to proclaim liberty to the captives and recovery of sight to the blind, to set at liberty those who are oppressed."

This was the mission for which Jesus had been sent: to preach, to heal, and to set free. All to bring glory to God the Father.

And again, in John 6:38 (NKJV), Jesus talked about being sent:

"For I have come down from heaven, not to do my own will, but the will of him who sent me."

In fact, there are twenty-six times in the Gospel of John alone where Jesus said that he had been sent by the Father. All of Jesus' life was about this "sent-ness." Sent by the Father to "seek and to save that which was lost."

However, mission work didn't start with Jesus. "Sent-ness" didn't start with Jesus. It's actually a theme that runs throughout the Bible. From Genesis to Revelation, God the Father is described as a sending God. He creates and then sends Adam and Eve into the garden. He sends Noah to build an ark. He sends Abraham to the land of Canaan. He sends Moses to Egypt. He sends Joshua and the people of Israel into the Promised Land. He sent judges to help rescue Israel from their enemies. He sent kings and prophets to the people of Israel. He sent armies against Israel as judgment. Finally, he sends Jesus.

This is the story of the Bible. This is the story of God. It's the story of a God who sends his people out on mission. From this story of a God who sent Jesus on mission, what do we see? What do we learn about the way of Jesus and mission?

It was Planned.

The Bible tells us that, from before the beginning of time, the mission of Jesus was all a part of God's plan. Ephesians 3:11 (ASV) speaks of God's plan:

"According to the eternal purpose which he purposed in Christ Jesus our Lord."

There are many other passages that use this same language of God's eternal purpose and plan in Jesus. What that tells us is that his salvation plan of Jesus and the cross was no afterthought. It was no plan B when plan A didn't work out. When Adam and Eve blew it in the garden, that original sin didn't create some cosmic crisis that left God surprised and confused.

No, this was the plan.

Jesus was it.

There was no other way.

It was Bethlehem's stable to Calvary's cross. It was swaddling clothes to grave clothes.

The implication of that is a big "wow." Any serious and thoughtful look at what Jesus suffered on the cross leaves us shaking our heads, thinking and wishing that surely there must have been another way.

There must be a better way.

There must be an easier way.

There must be a cheaper way.

There must be a bloodless way without pain and without sacrifice.

Even Jesus himself seemed to have struggled with this, because there, in the garden, just hours before his arrest, Jesus prayed, *"Father, if it be possible, let this cup pass from me; nevertheless, not as I will, but as you will."*

Since this was God's plan from the beginning, it's safe to say there was no other way for God's glory to be restored and God's people to be redeemed. This was the only way. And because this was the only way, we can also say that this was the best way. The cross was the best way. Let that sink in for a moment.

It was the way for God's wrath and hatred of sin to be settled once and for all.

It was the way for God to punish sin but love the sinner.

It was the way for God to be both righteous and forgiving.

It was the way for God's love to win.

It was all through the cross.

There was no plan B.

It was Promised.

Since the mission of Jesus was God's plan from the beginning, you would expect to find hints of that plan in the pages of Scripture. And what you expect is exactly what you find.

The Old Testament is full of the foreshadowing of what we see in Jesus.

- In Genesis, he is the woman's seed that would bruise the head of the serpent, and he is the ram that is provided in place of Abraham's son, Isaac.
- In Exodus, he is Moses who is sent back to Egypt to liberate God's people, the spotless lamb of the first Passover in Egypt, and the tent of meeting where Moses meets with God face to face.
- In Leviticus, he is the offerings and sacrifices.
- In Numbers, he is the bronze serpent on a pole.
- In Joshua, he is the "Commander of the Lord's Army" who meets with Joshua.
- In Judges, he is the many judges whom God raised up to defend his people.
- In Ruth, he is Boaz who claims a bride in Ruth.
- In Psalms, he is the one who cries out, "My God, my God, why have you forsaken me?"
- In Isaiah, he is the one whose name would be called "Wonderful, Counselor, Mighty God, Everlasting Father, Prince of Peace," the rod from the stem of Jesse, and the one who is "wounded for our transgres-

sions and bruised for our iniquities."
- In Jeremiah, he is the new covenant written on our hearts.
- In Ezekiel, he is the True Shepherd of Israel and the new city and new temple.
- In Micah, he is the ruler from Bethlehem Ephrathah.
- In Zechariah, he is the king of Jerusalem who comes riding on a donkey.
- In Malachi, he is the Lord who suddenly appears in his temple.

These are but a few of the glimpses we see of Jesus in the Old Testament. According to one source, there are 127 Messianic predictions in 3,000 different verses found in the Old Testament.

The promise of Jesus is there. The promise of his mission to redeem and restore is all there.

All you have to do is look. When you look, you will be filled with wonder.

It was Messy.

Jesus' mission and ministry were often messy. Simply put, Jesus never isolated himself or insulated himself from the mess and pain and brokenness of the world and culture around him. In fact, he would often go looking for the mess. Just look at the company he kept. They were a mess. They were common fishermen, tax collectors, and political zealots.

They were like Zacchaeus in Luke Chapter 19, a chief

tax collector who had become rich by stealing people's money. If you grew up in Sunday School, you probably remember singing about this "wee little man."

Zacchaeus was hated by every person he had ever cheated and robbed. But, in Luke 19:5, Jesus stepped right into this man's mess by inviting himself over for dinner.

"Zacchaeus, hurry and come down, for I must stay at your house today."

Surprise! It was a dinner that changed Zach's life.

As I mentioned before, Jesus encountered another guy whose life was so messed up that the only name of this man given in Scripture is "Legion." He was possessed by a legion of demons, and as a result, he lived in a cemetery, wore no clothes, and had the superhuman strength to break chains that bound him. It doesn't get messier than that. As the disciples huddled in fear of this guy, Jesus calmly told the demons to get lost and allowed them to enter a herd of pigs. (It didn't end well for the pigs or the demons.)

The next thing we see of "Legion" is that he is clothed, healed, free, and wanting to join the disciples in following Jesus. But Jesus does a curious thing. This guy would have been a huge attraction for "Team Jesus." This guy would have been a real asset to the team in sharing his story and pointing others to Jesus. Today, this guy would be invited to churches and conferences to give his testimony. His book would be a bestseller.

But what did Jesus do? Jesus sends him home.

In Mark 5:19, Jesus said:

"Go home to your friends and tell them how much the Lord has done for you and how he has had mercy on you."

Jesus sent him home. Jesus gave him a mission. As a result, Legion became the first missionary of the church age.

One more example is that of the "woman at the well." In John 4:4, there is an odd verse that says, *"And he had to pass through Samaria."*

This is worth noting because Jews didn't pass through Samaria. They went completely around Samaria. Jews avoided Samaria because they considered the Samaritans to be traitors and wanted nothing to do with them. Samaritans were "those people," but Jesus "had to pass through Samaria." Jesus was looking for someone, and that someone was a woman that he met at a public water well. As it turns out, her life was a mess too.

In John 4:18, when Jesus asks her about her husband, the woman answers, *"I have no husband."* Jesus said to her, *"You are right in saying, 'I have no husband.' For you have had five husbands, and the one you now have is not your husband."*

Jesus cut through the makeup right down to the mess. She had come to the well for water. She left the well that day with so much more.

This was the pattern of mission and ministry for Jesus. He went looking for the messy places, the broken places, the dark places of life. He was not afraid of getting his hands dirty with the people who needed him the most.

In Luke 5:31-32, Jesus said,

"Those who are well have no need of a physician, but those who are sick. I have not come to call the righteous, but sinners to repentance."

In calling sinners to repentance, Jesus got his hands dirty. That's the way of Jesus and mission. It was costly.

What did it cost Jesus to be a missionary? *Everything.*

It cost him leaving what he had enjoyed for all eternity past with the Father and the Spirit. That was "home" for Jesus. That was glory and power and perfection and beauty to a degree that we cannot even comprehend. He gave up heaven. Try to imagine that. Try to imagine the humility and self-sacrifice in that one dimension of Jesus as missionary.

Think of it like this. Imagine that all you have ever driven in your adult life is a Mercedes Benz. Imagine you've only driven this luxury car with the finest of materials, the latest technology, and the smoothest of rides. Sounds pretty good, right? Then, because of some type of severe financial setback, imagine if all you could afford was a bicycle, and not even a nice bicycle, but a used, single speed, rusted, hand-me-down. Maybe that's a little, just a little, of what it was like for Jesus to live as we live.

Paul tried to express this truth in Philippians 2:5-7 (NKJV) when he said:

"Let this mind be in you which was also in Christ Jesus, who,

83

being in the form of God, did not consider it robbery to be equal with God, but made Himself of no reputation, taking the form of a bondservant, and coming in the likeness of men."

Part of this incredible story of the gospel is the story of God becoming a servant.

Who would do such a thing? Who would even think of such a thing?

Only Jesus.

When Jesus became that servant, made of flesh and blood, that too was costly. It cost him to live as we live. Flesh and blood living is not easy—or painless. Jesus became a baby that grew into a boy and then a man. And along the way, he got hurt, stubbed his toes, got sick, became hungry, lost sleep, along with a thousand other aches and pains and discomforts that come with life as we know it to be.

Some will say, "Yes, but Jesus was God." True. But, he was also human. He willingly and even joyfully submitted himself to paying the cost for it.

Of course, the greatest cost was the cross. Words don't even come close to describing such a cost. It was first a physical cost of suffering. Romans were professional killers and had lots of practice. They knew exactly what to do in order to make death by crucifixion as painful as possible. In fact, crucifixion was such a horrible death that Roman citizens were protected by law from being crucified. It was a form of execution reserved for the worst of criminals, used to make examples out of those who defied Roman rule and authority. Ultimately, death for the crucified would only come from asphyxiation. Such suffering could continue for hours, if not days. This is the death that Jesus endured.

The cost was also spiritual. Scripture teaches us that, while on the cross, Jesus became our sin.

Isaiah 53:5-6 (NKJV), which by the way was written some 800 years before Jesus, tells us:

"But He was wounded for our transgressions, He was bruised for our iniquities; the chastisement for our peace was upon Him, and by His stripes we are healed. All we like sheep have gone astray; we have turned, every one, to his own way; and the Lord has laid on Him the iniquity of us all."

Did you catch that? Our iniquity was laid on him. We can see the same thing in 2 Corinthians 5:21 (NKJV):

"For He made Him who knew no sin to be sin for us, that we might become the righteousness of God in Him."

Did you catch that as well? Jesus became our sin. And not just some sin, but all of our sin, down to the last bitter drop of every foul thing you and I can imagine or do.

Why did Jesus do it? Love.

Jesus himself said it best in John 15:13:

"Greater love has no one than this, that someone lay down his life for his friends."

Of course, many have done exactly that. Heroes and saints have laid down their lives for the benefit of others all through history.

Among the many heroes of 9/11 were the passengers on Flight 93. Upon learning what the hijacked planes were being used for, they decided they were not going to be another one. They decided that evil would not succeed. They decided that, whatever the cost, they had to do something—even if it meant they would not survive.

"Greater love has no one than this."

What makes the cross different is that Jesus was no ordinary man, no mere mortal like you and me. This was God himself—infinite, all powerful, eternal. Yet, he stooped so low as to allow himself to be nailed to a rough, blood-stained cross. Then, he hung there, probably naked, for all the world to see and mock, yet praying for those who put him there until he took his last breath.

This was his mission. This is why he came into our world.

Who would do such a thing? Who could even conceive of such a thing? Only Jesus.

It was Successful.

The mission of Jesus did not end on the cross. It would be a mistake and short of the full gospel to see the cross as the end-all of his mission. The mission of Jesus was simply put on pause for three days. Three days later, Jesus was raised from the dead. The tomb could not hold him.

Death could not hold him. He had won.

He then appeared to his disciples. He taught them the Scriptures so that they finally began to understand the gospel. And then he sent them out to "go and make disciples of all the nations."

How did the disciples respond? They were fearless. Before the resurrection, they were cowards, hiding and running for their lives. Seeing Jesus and knowing Jesus was alive changed everything.

The Book of Acts tells their story. Someone once said that the Book of Acts can be outlined and understood in three simple ways: Jesus went up, the Holy Spirit came down, the Church went out. That is exactly what happened. They scattered, and everywhere they went, they were telling the good news that Jesus was alive.

And now, some 2,000 years later, the Church is still going out with the gospel. The mission of Jesus is now the mission of the Church—to take the gospel to every nation, every tribe, every language, every people group, in every corner of the globe. Because there are still those who have yet to hear the message that Jesus is alive.

Our Mission.

Now, the mission of Jesus is our mission. We are called to finish what Jesus started. We are called to be his hands and feet. Just as Jesus was sent by the Father, we too have been sent—by no less than Jesus himself.

In John 20:21, Jesus said:

"As the Father has sent me, even so I am sending you."

Now, *we* are the sent ones. And that isn't just for the special few. It's not just for the pastors and missionaries among us. It's for all of us. There are no exceptions and no exemptions for those who follow Jesus.

And what have we been sent to do? In Matthew 28:19-20, Jesus tells us exactly what he commands us to do.

"Go therefore and make disciples of all nations, baptizing them in the name of the Father and of the Son and of the Holy Spirit, teaching them to observe all that I have commanded you. And behold, I am with you always, to the end of the age."

Our mission is to make disciples who are baptized believers and followers of Jesus, who obey all that Jesus has taught, and then who can, in turn, make other disciples. In other words, our mission is to teach others to believe and follow Jesus in order to become more like Jesus.

All of us might not be called to another country or to the unreached nations, but we are all called to *go*. Even if that means going across the street. In your city, there are tens of thousands, if not millions, who need to hear and see the message of Jesus.

They are in your community. They are in your neighborhood. They are on your street. They may be next door.

Jesus said, "Go and make disciples." Right along with that plan, there is also a promise.

In the Old Testament, Jesus was a "one-day" promise. He was the promise that one day he would come and make all things new. But his promise to us now is different.

Again, in Matthew 28:20, Jesus said, *"And behold, I am with you always, to the end of the age."*

His promise is to be with us. Jesus has not left us. Jesus is right here, right now.

He knew we couldn't do this on our own. As a result, Jesus has sent us a helper, his Holy Spirit—who comforts, strengthens, equips, convicts the world of sin, and who points the world to Jesus.

In the Book of Acts, we read about how important the Holy Spirit is for this mission of making disciples.

In Acts 1:4-5, Jesus told his disciples:

"And while staying with them He ordered them not to depart from Jerusalem, but to wait for the promise of the Father, which, He said, 'you heard from me; for John baptized with water, but you will be baptized with the Holy Spirit not many days from now.'"

"Wait, you want us to wait?"

That's not what anyone expected. They were fired up and ready to go.

Like a football team after the coach's pep talk, they knew Jesus was alive and they were not afraid of anything.

It was game on.

As ready as they surely must have been, Jesus told them to wait. It was because they lacked one thing—*him*. They lacked the Holy Spirit who would live in them and fill them and fuel them for this mission of making disciples.

When the Holy Spirit did show up just a few days later, he blew it up. That very day, as a result of hearing the gospel from Peter, over 3,000 people became followers of Jesus. That is the power and potential of the Holy Spirit. That is the reason Jesus told them to wait for his Spirit to come.

And, this is the promise for us still today. It is the promise of the Holy Spirit who comes to live within the heart and life of every believer who follows Jesus. He is not optional. He is not conditional. If you love and follow Jesus, he lives within you, and it's only through and by and with his presence and power that we can "go and make disciples of all the nations." He is our fuel for missions, a fuel that is available for every believer and follower of Jesus. That is why you and I need to develop the habit of being filled with the Spirit every single day.

In Ephesians 5:18, Paul wrote, *"And do not get drunk with wine, for that is debauchery, but be filled with the Spirit."*

Paul writes like this because, even though every believer has been given the Spirit, we tend to leak. And because we leak and let other things control us and distract us from the mission of making disciples, we need to develop the habit of being filled back up with the Spirit of God.

It's like the car you drive. After a fill-up, sooner or later, the gas needle drops to empty. And the more you drive, the sooner it happens. My wife often accuses me of trying to drive on fumes. I admit it. I'm guilty.

But we don't have to drive on fumes with the Holy

Spirit. He is always there and always ready to fill us and empower us for the work that Jesus has given us.

The mission of making disciples will be messy. That is because you have to meet people where they are in their current condition, not with how you wish they would be.

For a number of years, I had the honor of leading our church in a ministry to homeless people in downtown Mobile, Alabama. Once a month, we would drive to a local shelter to cook and serve a meal for those living on the streets. It was often a messy and smelly experience. So many of the people we met were broken and bruised by life. But, I always left with the feeling that this is exactly what Jesus had called us to do.

Too often in the Western church today we want to "clean the fish before we catch the fish." But, that doesn't really work well, does it? Before you can clean them, you have to catch them.

Discipleship begins with catching the fish and only then continues with the long process of helping to clean them. I say, "helping to clean them," because only the Holy Spirit can actually do the cleaning. He is the one who transforms and changes someone to be more and more like Jesus, but he uses other believers in the process.

Think about what your life was like before following Jesus. Mine was a mess and yours probably was, too. Now, with the prevalence of drugs, booze, pornography, divorce, and addiction of all kinds, the mess has only gotten worse, which means the brokenness has gotten worse as well.

Dear reader, our world is broken, but Jesus calls us into

that world to be the salt and the light in a dark and dying world. It will be messy. Your hands will get dirty. Your heart will be broken. But that's the way of Jesus.

The mission of making disciples will be costly. In fact, Jesus actually had a lot to say about the cost of following him. He warned potential followers about the cost of following him. He warned them with words like, *"If anyone would come after Me, let him deny himself and take up his cross and follow Me."*

He warned them with words like, *"If anyone comes to Me and does not hate his own father and mother and wife and children and brothers and sisters, yes, and even his own life, he cannot be My disciple."*

He warned them with words like, *"Then they will deliver you up to tribulation and put you to death, and you will be hated by all nations for My names sake."*

Jesus warned the rich young ruler, *"You lack one thing: go, sell all that you have and give to the poor, and you will have treasure in heaven; and come, follow me."*

That is all pretty heavy stuff.

Jesus wanted them—and us—to know the truth.

What truth? There is a price to pay in following Jesus.

Okay, so here is the problem. We don't see that being taught in most of our Western churches today. In most of our churches, there is a nod and a wink to what Jesus said, but then we continue to live like the rest of the culture around us. We like Jesus and we want to follow Jesus as long as it doesn't cost us anything.

How else can you explain the statistic that the average

church goer gives only 3 percent of their income to the mission of the church and then goes out and drives home in 50,000-dollar vehicles? How else can you explain that we spend more on our pets than we do on world missions? How else can you explain pastors who brag about their Rolex watches and pastors who raise money for a private jet?

How does that look like Jesus? How does that obey Jesus?

Lord, help us.

Lord, convict us.

Lord, change us.

What is needed today are people who are willing to pay any price in order to follow Jesus into the mission that he has given us. What is needed today are men and women who believe that it is "more blessed to give than to receive" and who live that way. Those who are willing to wake up from the American dream of a nice job, a nice retirement, a nice car, and a nice house in order to follow Jesus into the world to make disciples.

I personally dream of a time for my generation of Baby Boomers when, instead of retiring and possibly chasing little white balls around a golf course somewhere, we would become a missionary army. Yes, we could become an army, invading and pushing back the darkness in places near and far. Why not? Why not trade in a golf cart for an ox cart? Why not trade in your "golden years" for your best years of reaching others and teaching others the gospel? No other generation in history will have more time, more resources, better health, or longer lifespans, than our generation of

Baby Boomers.

May I gently remind you of what Jesus said in Luke 12:48, *"Everyone to whom much is given, of him much will be required."*

We have been given so much. Jesus promises that he will require much. Now, it's time to give back.

I was recently reminded of the message that John Piper gave at the One Day Passion Conference on May 20, 2000. In that message, Piper shared the story of Ruby Eliason and Laura Edwards.

This is what he said: "Three weeks ago we got word at our church that Ruby Eliason and Laura Edwards had both been killed in Cameroon. Ruby was over 80. Laura was a widow, a medical doctor, pushing 80 years old, and serving at Ruby's side in Cameroon. The brakes failed, the car went over the cliff, and they were both killed instantly. And I asked my people: was that a tragedy? Two lives, driven by one great vision, spent in unheralded service to the perishing poor for the glory of Jesus Christ—two decades after almost all their American counterparts have retired to throw their lives away on trifles in Florida or New Mexico. No. That is not a tragedy. That is glory."

How are you spending your life? How are you using your resources? What are you chasing? Will your life end up in the tragedy of trivial pursuits and totally waste what you have been given, or will you invest what you have in making disciples that bring glory to God?

I'm calling you out.

You can do this. Just follow Jesus.

The Way of Jesus
Questions for the Journey

Chapter Five "Jesus and Mission"

Read Luke 19:10. What was Jesus sent to do?

Charles Spurgeon said, "Every believer is either a missionary or an imposter." Was he right? Why?

What have we been sent to do?

Do you see yourself as a missionary?
Why or why not?

What would need to change in your life in order to live life on mission like Jesus?

Where could you be a missionary right now?

Chapter Six
The Way of Jesus and Love

Jesus wept. (John 11:35)

I know, I know…everyone wants to talk or write or sing about the love of Jesus. It seems that just about everyone, right down to atheists and agnostics, can agree on this one thing: Jesus was an example of love and compassion. That's why so many can and do admire Jesus while living outside any connection with him.

There are many who, like Mahatma Gandhi, admire Jesus, but marvel that Christians are so unlike their Christ. For many, there is a disconnect between the Jesus they see in the Bible and the Jesus they see in the church. Because what do we see of Jesus in the Bible?

John 11:35 is one of those Bible verses that was every kid's favorite in Sunday School. It was a favorite, not for its theology or doctrine, but because it was the shortest and therefore the easiest to memorize.

"Sure, I can quote the Bible—*Jesus wept.*"

But, what we used to laugh at as a joke has now become to me and many others something beautiful. I believe this verse should still be our favorite verse; not because it's short, but because it's deep. There are no other words used together in Scripture that take us deeper into the heart of God than these two simple words.

Let's look at the context of the verse.

John Chapter 11 tells the story of Jesus and his disciples receiving word that a close friend named Lazarus was sick and that his two sisters, Martha and Mary, were worried and asking Jesus for help. And why not? They had seen Jesus heal others so, surely, he would heal his friend.

But, instead of rushing to their side, Jesus waited…and waited…and waited. Jesus waited for four long days before making the journey to see his friends. By the time Jesus arrived in Bethany where Lazarus and his sisters lived, Lazarus had already died and been buried. When Jesus does arrive, they take him to Lazarus' tomb, and when Jesus sees the mourners, the friends, and the family there at the burial site, Jesus begins to weep. The tears begin to flow. Jesus needs a Kleenex. Maybe he needs a box of Kleenex.

You may be thinking *What's the big deal? Everyone cries.* First, remember who this was. Jesus was God who had clothed himself in flesh and blood. He and the Father were one. Jesus was the enigma where God continues to be God but also becomes one of us. He is Emmanuel which means "God with us," but in John 11:35, "God with us" is a mess of emotion.

Take a moment to frame a snapshot of this in your mind. Don't let it go just yet. Try to picture this. Can you hear his sobs? Can you see the tears? What does this mean about Jesus?

I believe it can only be explained by realizing that Jesus was also a friend. Lazarus was a friend. Mary and Martha were his friends, which meant their grief was now his grief. Their sorrow was now his sorrow—in spite of the fact that Jesus was about to turn everyone's sorrow into joy by raising Lazarus from the dead. Mourning was about to turn into dancing. Crying was about to turn into singing. But, before the miracle and before the joy, there was the grief and there were tears.

Tears of emotion are unique to us as humans. Other creatures, even crocodiles, shed tears, but our tears are special. Tears of emotion are a window to the soul. As humans, we only cry tears of emotion for the things that are important to us. We cry over what we love. And it was no different for Jesus. He loved Mary, Martha, and Lazarus.

John 11:36 (MEV) goes on to quote those at the tomb that day saying of Jesus, *"Look at how he loved him."*

He loved the Father.

He loved his family.

He loved his disciples.

He loved the children who were brought to him.

He even loved those who chose not to follow him.

If actions are more powerful than words, it would be safe to say that Jesus loved all those he healed and fed, and even those he rebuked for their hardness of hearts.

Of course, the greatest demonstration of Jesus' love was yet to come.

In the movie, *The Passion of the Christ*, it's said that the hands that portrayed a Roman soldier's hands driving the nails into Jesus' wrist were in fact the hands of director Mel Gibson.

But, it wasn't the Romans who nailed Jesus to the cross, nor Jewish hands that nailed Jesus to the cross. It was love that nailed Jesus to the cross.

Each blow of the hammer with its iron on iron was the work and wonder of love. First, love for the Father, and then it was love for us. It was what former Catholic priest and author Brennan Manning once referred to as "the furious love of God."

It was furious as opposed to shallow.

It was furious as opposed to fake.

It was furious as opposed to half-hearted.

This was and still is the love of Christ, and nowhere do you see that portrayed better than at the cross, where furious love met grievous sin—and love won.

The Love of Jesus

How did Jesus love the people around him? What were the marks of that furious love? A good place to start would be to see how Jesus pursued those he loved. Jesus never waited for people to come to him. He pursued relationships and pursued opportunities to love those around him.

When Jesus met a tax collector named Zacchaeus, Jesus could have simply ignored this little man who had climbed up a tree in order to catch a glimpse of Jesus, but instead of ignoring him, what did Jesus do? He invited himself to this man's house for dinner. That might not have been polite, but love is not always polite.

Another mark of how Jesus loved those around him was that Jesus always called those around him to become better than what they were before. Jesus didn't let Simon Peter settle for being a fisherman. Jesus called him to be a "fisher of men." He didn't even let Simon settle for just being "Simon" but later changed his name to "Peter," which means "rock." Because, on the rock of Peter's confession of faith, Jesus would build his Church.

Jesus didn't let the rich young man just settle for keeping the commandments but rather called him to go and sell his riches and give them to the poor and then follow him.

Another mark of the love of Jesus was that Jesus served those around him. In John Chapter 13, as referenced earlier, Jesus took a towel and a pan of water and washed the feet of his disciples. It was an act so shocking that Peter objected and almost refused to participate. In John 13:8 (MEV) Peter says, *"You shall never wash my feet."*

Only lowly slaves washed people's feet—along with those who truly know how to love someone enough to become their servant.

Another mark of the love of Jesus was that Jesus forgave those he loved. The real test of the love of Jesus (and the patience of Jesus) was that group of twelve men he called as his disciples. During their three years together, it appears that Jesus had to forgive these men again and again. They were hard of heart and slow to believe. Yet, even after running away from him and denying him, Jesus was quick to forgive.

A final mark of the love of Jesus was, of course, how he gave himself for those he loved. Again, the cross is the ultimate example of what the love of Jesus was all about. But Jesus didn't just preach that kind of love. He lived it in order to show us what real love looks like.

The Eleventh Commandment

For those who follow Jesus to become more like Jesus, we are commanded to love like he loved. If you follow Jesus, you actually follow eleven commandments. There are the first ten that we find in Exodus Chapter 20 that were given through Moses to the people of Israel. These, of course, were the "big ten." They were the gold standard for Judaism since Moses came down from Mount Sinai with the commandments freshly engraved by the hand of God himself.

But, in John 13:34, Jesus adds one to the list:

A" new commandment I give to you, that you love one another; just as I have loved you, you also are to love one another."

Right up there with the worship of God and God alone, keeping the Sabbath, and the other eight commandments, Jesus adds the commandment to love one another. It is remarkable in both the authority Jesus assumes (only God can give commandments) and in the action that he expects. For Jesus, nothing less than a new commandment would do.

Did you notice in that verse who we are to love? We are to love *one another*. There is no guess work here. There are no question marks here. If there is any one thing that we are to be known for in the church, it is this one thing.

Yes, he means those people who sit next to you each Sunday. He means those people across the room who have not spoken to you in weeks. He means those leaders you disagree with and who hurt your feelings. Yes, he means *those* people. In fact, in the very next verse, Jesus goes on to say: *"By this shall all men know that you are my disciples, if you have love for one another."*

Clearly, according to Jesus, the one identifying mark of the Christian is our love for one another.

Dear reader, if the church you attend is not ruled and led by love for each other, then it might be a great group of people with great music and great organization, but it is not a church.

I have always been impressed with what Jesus could have said and could have used as the true mark of a disciple. It could have been theology. It could have been doctrine. It could have been generosity. It could have been purity. It could have been worship. It could have been obedience to the Law of Moses. It could have been any number of things that we substitute for love, and all too often, we love our substitutes rather than loving each other.

Oh, how we love our substitutes.

Here is the great weakness of the Western church today. We substitute everything else for love. The reason for that is simple…substitutes are easy. It's easy to claim to be a reformed, premillennial, charismatic, Bible-believing, worship-loving, evangelical Christian, but loving one another…not so much.

Loving each other is hard and it gets messy at times. It means getting our hands dirty and our hearts broken. As a result, many do not even try. That's why the name on the outside of the building may say "church," but what's on the inside says something completely different. Many of you know exactly what I mean.

If that were not enough, did you notice how we are to love one another. Read the verse again. Come on, say it with me. We are to love one another *as Jesus loves us*. His love for us is the standard. His love for us is the bar that we are called to reach. In other words, we are not commanded just to "like" each other in the church or endure each other. We are called to the same love that Jesus has for us that pursues, encourages, forgives, serves, and gives itself away. This is to be the beauty and the blessing of the church.

Why love? Why is this to be the one true mark of a follower of Jesus? Surely it must have something to do with the nature and character of the Father.

First John 4:8 (MEV) reminds us that *"Anyone who does not love does not know God, because God is love."*

Love is the very essence of the nature and character of God. Therefore, when we love one another as Jesus loves us, we are unveiling the reality of God. Loving one another is like God putting on skin—our skin.

Another reason must surely be that love is what the world needs most to see and to know.

The Beatles reminded us of this way back in 1967 with their hit song "All You Need is Love." Of course, the world needs more than just love, but loving one another the way Jesus loves us would certainly go a long, long way in making the world a better place.

A final reason must surely be that love has to start in the church. Think about it. If you cannot love someone sitting next to you in a church who looks like you and talks like you and lives like you, how in the world will you love someone out in the world who is different from you? Guess what, you cannot and will not.

I love the story that I came across many years ago in a long-forgotten book. The story is of the Apostle John as he lived out the last of his days in the city of Ephesus. It is said that, on every Lord's Day, John would be carried to attend the local church there. He had to be carried because he was so old and could no longer walk. Every time John was present, he would be asked to say a few words. And why not? He was John the Apostle. But every time John spoke, he would always say the same thing, "Little children, love one another." Finally, the day came when someone in the church asked him, "John, why is it that every time we ask you to speak to us you always say the same thing?" It is said that John's response was, "It is the Lord's command, and if this alone be done, it is enough."

The story may just be a church tradition or legend, but it certainly sounds like Jesus, and it also sounds like what John would say.

The Cost of Love

When you love the way Jesus loves you, it's not going to be easy. Just look at Jesus. When you love the way Jesus loves you, there will always be a risk. It can and probably will break your heart, just as it did for Jesus.

C.S. Lewis once said, "To love at all is to be vulnerable. Love anything, and your heart will certainly be wrung and possibly broken. If you want to make sure of keeping it intact you must give it to no one, not even an animal. Wrap it carefully round with hobbies and little luxuries; avoid all entanglements. Lock it up safe in the casket or coffin of your selfishness. But in that casket, safe, dark, motionless, airless, it will change. It will not be broken; it will become unbreakable, impenetrable, irredeemable. To love is to be vulnerable. The only place outside of Heaven where you can be perfectly safe from all the dangers and perturbations of love is Hell."

Just three weeks before writing this chapter, we got the news that no one ever wants to get.

Ten years ago, on my first mission trip to Guatemala, I met a little three-year-old Mayan Achi boy in a village way up in the mountains. His name was Rudy. He seemed to be just like all the other little boys of that village, but then

I heard his story.

His birth mother had given him up at birth and had no contact with him. He had spent several months as a baby in the hospital, and, during that time, was all alone. In later years, his extended family did their best to take care of Rudy, but they had families of their own to take care of.

After hearing his story that week, my wife and I began a ten-year journey of helping to care for Rudy. We would have adopted Rudy, but soon after meeting him, Guatemala closed their adoption program due to so many abuses in the system. That door was closed to us. But, with every yearly visit to Guatemala, we got to visit with Rudy. It was always the highlight of our ministry time in Guatemala

When Rudy was old enough for school, we started sending money to help with clothes and supplies. Then, with the help of family and friends, we were able to move Rudy to live with a dear friend who loved him as much as we did. After a year with her, we then moved Rudy to live with Mary Purvis, a missionary working there in Guatemala. Living with her, Rudy was safe, well fed, and in school. It was all for Rudy. It was all so that he would know he was loved and that he would be given a chance at a better life.

Finally, when Sally and I knew that God was calling us to live and serve in Costa Rica, we were able to make arrangements for Rudy and his half-sister, Belsy, to come and live with us there. It was one glorious year together when they just got to be kids. They were safe, they were loved, they were fed (Rudy loved to eat—a lot), they were in school, and they were serving with us in our church. It was a year filled with so many great memories. I wish I could share each and every one of them with you.

But then, when we arrived back in Costa Rica for our second year, Rudy and Belsy had been back in Guatemala spending time with family, and as a result, decided to stay there. I didn't want to make them return with us. It needed to be their decision, and they decided to stay. That was the first time our hearts were broken but not the last.

Again, just three weeks before writing this chapter, late one Friday night, we received a phone call from our daughter, Leah, back in the States that our missionary in Guatemala was trying to contact us because Rudy had been shot. Later that same night, we were told that some men had walked into the family's apartment and, for reasons that are still not clear to us, shot and killed our Rudy. He was just thirteen years old.

How do I describe that kind of pain? What words can I write that can heal what's been broken? What can help us understand why Rudy was taken from us? I am not there yet. I am not sure I will ever get there. But, this is the risk of love.

It would have been so much easier to not get attached and not get involved. It would have been easier to close my heart and look the other way. I could have ignored my concern for Rudy years ago with, "He is not my responsibility, let someone else take care of this kid."

Yeah, that would have been easier, safer, and certainly cheaper. But oh, what we would have missed.

Rudy's first bicycle.

Rudy's new clothes.

Rudy's phone calls.

Rudy's first trip to the States for Christmas.

Rudy's second trip to the States for Christmas.

Rudy's birthday when he did a face-plant in his birthday cake thanks to our friend David Sharpless.

Rudy's homework.

Rudy's appetite.

Rudy's soccer games.

Rudy's baptism.

Rudy's prayers.

These are all the things we would have never experienced if we had not chosen to love our Rudy.

Was it worth it? Absolutely.

Wherever you are today, you can choose to live in a bubble. You can choose to play it safe and not put your heart out there where it might get broken. You can lock it away and then throw away the key. You can just look the other way and keep your heart safe, sealed, and protected. But each time you make that choice, your heart will shrivel and shrink. You always lose what you do not use. Don't lose it.

Yes, love is risky. Yes, love is hard. It will cost you something to love others.

No one knows that any better than Jesus.

The Way of Jesus
Questions for the Journey

Chapter Six "Jesus and Love"

How did Jesus love those around Him?

What is the eleventh commandment?

Why is love to be the "mark" of a follower of Jesus?

Love for others springs from and flows out of
our being loved. Do you know that you are loved?

How have you experienced God's love in your life?

Read 1 Corinthians 13:1-7. How does the
Bible describe real love for others?

Where do you see that love in your life?

Who are you being called to love?
What should that look like?

Chapter Seven
The Way of Jesus and Suffering

Consider him who endured from sinners such hostility against himself, so that you may not grow weary or fainthearted.
(Hebrews 12:3)

This is the way of Jesus that I struggle with most. Truth be told, I'd rather not even have to write about it. No one likes the idea of suffering. No one wants to experience suffering. We try to avoid and evade in every way possible.

However, that's not how we see Jesus respond to suffering. Throughout the Bible, we see that Jesus was familiar with the way of suffering. Even before he was born, the prophets spoke of Jesus' suffering. Some 800 years before Bethlehem, Isaiah 53:3-4 wrote:

"He was despised and rejected by men; a man of sorrows, and acquainted with grief; and as one from whom men hide their faces, He was despised and we esteemed Him not. Surely He has borne our griefs and carried our sorrows; yet we esteemed Him stricken, smitten by God, and afflicted."

How is that for a life story? Stricken, smitten, and afflicted.

History tells us that it's likely that Jesus' earthly father, Joseph, died at an early age. As the oldest son, Jesus was required to provide for his mother and family. At age thirty, Jesus begins his ministry as a vagabond teacher. Initially, his family thinks he is crazy. He often offends those around him, especially the religious. He is constantly on the move with little comforts. He has nowhere to rest. He is often in the crosshairs of criticism and suspicion. He weeps over unbelief. He lives at the point of exhaustion. He is rejected by many. He is betrayed by one of his own. He is abandoned and denied by his disciples. He is beaten almost to the point of death. He is spat upon and mocked. He is stripped of clothes and nailed to a cross. He becomes the horror of every foul thing that ever has or ever will be sin against a holy God. He is forsaken by God the Father. He suffers an agonizing death. He is then buried in a borrowed tomb.

His life was not easy. But what is so amazing to consider is that, as God Himself, Jesus did not have to submit to this kind of life. He had all the power and all the authority that he needed to turn water into wine, to turn a boy's sack lunch into a feast, and to raise the dead back to life.

So, he had the power to turn a life of suffering into a life of luxury.

But, he didn't.

On the contrary, Jesus ran toward suffering. He embraced suffering. When Jesus entered Jerusalem the final time—while riding a donkey—with the crowd shouting, "Hosanna"—he knew what the result would be.

And when he cleansed the temple from those who had made it a "den of thieves"—he knew payback was coming.

But even while embracing his own life of suffering, Jesus also ran to the suffering of others. It seems that, most of the time, Jesus was surrounded by broken, wounded, and hurting people. Rather than sending them away, Jesus was always quick to heal. These were the people he had come for. This was his mission. It was a life of suffering—not just for himself—but for those who surrounded him and were helped by him.

Is the way of suffering that we see in Jesus the way for all who follow Jesus? Can we expect to suffer as he did? We don't have to go far to find the answer.

- Consider the book of Job: Job lost everything he had but never lost his faith in God.
- Consider the book of Lamentations: A book of tears and bitter grief.
- Consider the prophets: They often spoke truth to power. Not many did that and got away with it.
- Consider the disciples: All but one died as martyrs for following Jesus.
- Consider the early church: At one point, many were scattered because of persecution.
- Consider Paul: He was beaten, stoned, shipwrecked, and often made a prison his home. He too died as a martyr for following Jesus.
- Consider that the Book of 1 Peter in the New Testament

was written for the purpose of comforting and encouraging believers who were suffering.

- Consider the first 300 years of the Church. Persecution was common and often brutal. Nero was said to have used Christians wrapped in animal skins and soaked in oil as torches to light the streets of Rome.
- Consider that there have been more Christian martyrs in the last century than all other centuries combined.
- Consider the plight of Christians today in countries like Iraq, Egypt, and Iran to name just a few.

What this tells us is that suffering is a normal part of life and part of following Jesus. Jesus shows us that real life happens not on the mountain top but in the valley. And some valleys are deeper and longer and darker than others.

There is the valley of death, the valley of failure, the valley of fear, the valley of depression, the valley of addiction, the valley of sickness—all deep and wide and dark. I've been to some of those valleys and chances are pretty good that you have, too. Suffering is a normal part of life. Jesus even tells us that suffering is to be expected.

In John 15:20, Jesus said:

"Remember the word that I said to you: 'a servant is not greater than his master. If they persecuted me, they will also persecute you.'"

What that means, dear reader, is that the way of Jesus

is the way of suffering. It is not a question of *if* you will suffer, but rather *when* you will suffer. It just comes with taking up your cross to follow Jesus and living in a sin-broken, messed up world. And for many of us in the West, suffering becomes the pin prick that God uses to bust our "good life" balloons.

Of course, there are those who will try to tell you something different. There are those who will tell you that God wants to protect you from suffering, and that the way of Jesus is the way of blessing, not suffering. It is the gospel of more—more money, more things, more happiness, more blessings—so that you can wear that Rolex watch, drive that new car, live in that new house, and fly first class. Be large and in charge. It can all be yours when you follow Jesus, they say. All it takes is the right kind of faith and the right size donation.

Baloney.

Heresy.

That is a different gospel than what we see in Jesus. The gospel that we see in Jesus is the gospel of less, the gospel of humility, the gospel of serving and suffering for the sake of others.

The Blessing of Suffering

Can there be blessings that come from suffering? Can good come out of what is bad? The way of Jesus tells us *yes*. The suffering of Jesus, in all of its pain and horror, was for a purpose—the Father's glory and our good. There was no other way or better way to repair and redeem what was broken. Jesus understood that.

Soon after the resurrection, Jesus appeared to two of his followers as they were walking on the road to Emmaus. They were heartbroken and defeated, but Jesus challenged them and encouraged them in Luke 24:25-26 by saying:

"O foolish ones, and slow of heart to believe all that the prophets have spoken. Was it not necessary that the Christ should suffer these things and enter into his glory?"

Did you catch the word "necessary?"

Jesus knew that there are some things that can only be gained and won by suffering.

And, it is no different today for you and me.

Just ask the professional athlete. Ask them how many days/months/years they have suffered in a smelly gym somewhere to get to where they are today.

Ask the surgeon how many years and how many hours they have invested while suffering through books on human anatomy so they could make the scalpel heal instead of hurt.

Ask the farmer how many long hours are spent out in the field suffering heat and cold while praying for the harvest to be the reward.

Some things can only be gained and won through suffering. In fact, I would go so far as to say that without suffering, we would know nothing of any real value.

Some years ago, I came across a poem by Robert

Browning Hamilton that helped me to see the truth about suffering.

> "I walked a mile with pleasure
> She chatted all the way,
> But left me none the wiser
> For all she had to say.
> I walked a mile with sorrow
> And ne'er a word said she;
> But oh the things I learned from her
> When sorrow walked with me."

I will be the first to admit that I do not think I have suffered much in my life—not in comparison to others. But, the seasons of suffering I have been through have been the seasons when I have grown and learned the most.

I have learned that life is short, and every day is a gift. I have learned that material things are worthless. I have learned that my family and friends are priceless. I have learned that this life is not all that there is and that the best is yet to come. I have learned that God's promises in his Word are all true. I have learned that he is with me and will never leave me. I have learned that I do not have to have all the answers. I have learned that the little things in life are really the big things.

Far from avoiding and evading suffering, learn to embrace it. There is something in suffering that can be learned no other way.

As C.S. Lewis once said, "God whispers to us in our pleasures, speaks in our consciences, but shouts in our pains. It is his megaphone to rouse a deaf world."

God is shouting because there is something important that he wants us to hear. We just need to be listening.

The Joy of Suffering

Come on, really? Can there really be joy in our suffering?

In Hebrews 12:2, the Bible says, *"Who for the joy that was set before him endured the cross, despising it's shame."*

But what joy could that be? What joy could there be in going to a cross and dying a horrible death? What joy could there be in Jesus becoming our sin and then becoming the punishment for our sin?

Perhaps it was the joy of completion. The cross finished the work that Jesus came to do. Jesus even said as much while on the cross with, *"It is finished."*

Think about the things that you have finished in your life—a job, a degree, a book, a race. It feels good to finish. Even now I know there will be joy when I finish this book. There is joy when you finish something.

Perhaps it was the joy of victory. The cross was going to look like defeat. It was going to look like just another misguided zealot leading a misguided movement of misguided people. But appearances would be deceiving. Jesus was going to take everything sin and hell were going to throw at him, and he would win. An empty tomb proved it.

At the very least, it was the joy of saving what had been lost—all of humanity. On a personal level, what had been lost was you and me and our ability to know and enjoy a relationship with the very one who had made us for himself. Jesus changed all that. Jesus saved us from what had been lost.

There would have been great joy in knowing what Jesus knew: *that the cross was about to change everything.*

But there are also other examples of joy in suffering in Scripture.

In Luke 6:22-23, in what is Luke's version of the Sermon on the Mount, Jesus says:

"Blessed are you when people hate you and when they exclude you and revile you and spurn your name as evil, on account of the Son of Man. Rejoice in that day, and leap for joy, for behold, your reward is great in heaven; for so their fathers did to the prophets."

Rejoice? Leap for joy? Yes.

That's what Jesus said because he knew that suffering for his sake here only leads to greater blessing there—in the life to come.

The apostles understood this and, after being arrested and beaten by the Jewish leaders, Acts 5:41 tells us that they *"left the presence of the council rejoicing that they were counted worthy to suffer dishonor for the Name."*

Dear reader, there is no greater joy than to suffer for the name of Jesus. Suffering for your own actions or the actions of others is one thing, but to suffer for just following Jesus is a unique honor that few have known.

One year while leading a mission team to Cuba, I

made the mistake of drinking an open glass of papaya juice at one of the nicest hotels in Havana. I used to love papaya, and this was a really nice restaurant at a respected hotel so I assumed it would be safe to drink. Wrong. Just a few hours later, in the middle of the night, my stomach woke me up and it was really angry that I drank that juice. I will spare you the details. To make matters worse, it was a travel day with flights ahead to get our team back to the States. At one point during that awful day—a day I would rather forget—I can remember feeling a sense of joy that I had been given the honor of suffering for the name and the work of Jesus. Even if it was my own fault for drinking that papaya. By the way, I can't stand the taste of papaya now. Just thought you might want to know.

Whether it's sickness or inconvenience or poverty, or something much worse like prison or death, there is joy in being counted worthy to suffer for the sake of the Name.

The Purpose of Suffering

There can be joy in suffering because a believer can realize that there is a purpose in our suffering.

That purpose led James, the half-brother of Jesus, to write in James 1:2-4:

"Count it all joy, my brothers, when you meet trials of various kinds, for you know that the testing of your faith produces steadfastness. And let steadfastness have its full effect, that you may be perfect and complete, lacking nothing."

In other words, James is telling us that suffering is the one thing that God uses above all others to test us and refine us and make us more like him. That is what this book is all about. That is what discipleship is all about—to become more like Jesus.

And for that reason, we can "count it all joy." We can choose joy. *Not bitterness, not anger, not hate.*

You and I can actually choose joy because it makes us more like Jesus.

Think of suffering like silver polish. When silver becomes tarnished, an ugly brown eventually hides an original beauty. It has something to do with the other metals in the silver that begin to react to oxygen, and tarnish is the result. And what does it take to polish silver? An abrasive. Put a little calcium carbonate on a rag, apply some elbow grease to it, and the silver begins to shine again.

There is little doubt that suffering is an abrasive. Ask anyone who has been there and done that. It hurts. It's painful. But it's exactly what God uses to make us shine, and only God knows how much to use and how long to polish us until all the tarnish is gone and the shine is back.

When suffering comes, and it will, just remember that God is doing some polishing, and, the more he polishes, the brighter you will be.

That's exactly why those who have suffered the most often seem to shine the brightest.

In fact, this is exactly what Paul teaches us in 2 Corinthians 4:17: *"For this light momentary affliction is preparing for us an eternal weight of glory beyond all comparison."*

Yes, suffering in the ways of Jesus prepares us and polishes us for something better. Paul calls it "an eternal weight of glory." We don't know what that will be, but it's going to be good.

My encouragement to you, dear reader, is to never waste your suffering. Yes, it hurts, and yes, it's hard, and it's something that you would rather not have to experience. Maybe there are tears right now as you feel the pain of what you are going through. Let the tears flow. Tears are good. Tears help us heal and help us feel all that we are going through. Remember, you only cry about the things that you love and care deeply about. So, let them flow, but also realize and remember that those tears are what God is using to water a garden. A garden of good things that he is teaching you and showing you through that suffering.

It is as Paul tells us in Romans 8:28 (NKJV): "*All things work together for good, for those who love God and are called according to his purpose.*"

Hang on, dear one. You will get through this. And when you do, you will be better because of it.

I want to also encourage you to expect suffering and embrace that suffering.

Remember, from James Chapter 1, it's our suffering that is making us "complete, lacking nothing." When you run from suffering and avoid suffering, you are actually running from the very thing that God wants to use to make you more like Jesus.

The End of Suffering

Now for the good news—suffering does not last. Jesus endured the cross for a limited amount of time, perhaps for a few hours, and then it was over. The same is true for us here and now. No matter what type of suffering you might endure, even if it's for the rest of your life, eventually, that suffering will not last. Suffering is for a season. It has an expiration date, and that is good news.

Scripture points us to a time, for those who follow Jesus, when suffering will be no more. Guess what? We know the end of the story. The story of Jesus and his kingdom has an amazing end when suffering, tears, and death itself will be no more.

Revelation 21:3-4 depicts it for us like this:

"And I heard a loud voice from the throne saying, 'Behold, the dwelling place of God is with man. He will dwell with them, and they will be his people, and God himself will be with them as their God. He will wipe away every tear from their eyes, and death shall be no more, neither shall there be mourning, nor crying, nor pain anymore, for the former things have passed away.'"

When you walk through suffering—and you will— try to picture and imagine what this will be like. Try to picture that God himself will wipe away your tears.

Dwell on that image.

Soak that in.

Rest in that thought.

As I write these words, it's raining here. It's not just a drizzle or even a shower, it's one of those Costa Rican downpours where the clouds turn dark and forget their manners. It's raining hard.

Sometimes, suffering can feel like that. A downpour of hurt. A burst of pain and tears. But those tears are not forever. It will not last. One day, the rain will be over, the clouds will part, the sun will shine, and you and I will stand before a loving Father. He will reach down, and with his gentle touch, wipe away those tears, that pain, that hurt. Every single one.

That sickness will be gone.

That disease will be healed.

That loss will be restored.

That dark place will be filled with light.

And, at long last, that suffering will be over.

Forever.

The Way of Jesus
Questions for the Journey

Chapter Seven "Jesus and Suffering"

Read Isaiah 53:3. Make a list of the words that Isaiah used to describe God's servant.

How is Isaiah 53:3 a picture of Jesus?

Should followers of Jesus expect to suffer? Why or why not?

What good can come out of suffering?

Think back over your life to this point.
What have you learned from suffering?

How have you seen blessing, joy, or purpose
in that suffering?

Chapter Eight
The Way of Jesus and Glory

Was it not necessary that the Christ should suffer these things and enter into His glory? (Luke 24:26)

To be clear, suffering was not the end of the story for Jesus. A cross and a tomb were not the end of the story for Jesus. The bad news is over. The winter has passed. Spring has come. Glory is where the story of Jesus ends.

The good news of Jesus tells us that, on the third day after Jesus was crucified and buried, there was a resurrection. The icy grip of death had melted. Death did not have the last word. The grave was no match for the one it tried to contain. Jesus stepped out of that tomb alive and then appeared to his disciples and to many others over the next forty days. The entire gospel of Jesus Christ rests on this one essential part of the story of Jesus—an empty tomb.

The Apostle Paul described it like this in I Corinthians 15:3-8:

"I passed on to you what was most important and what had also been passed on to me. Christ died for our sins, just as the Scriptures said. He was buried, and He was raised from the dead on the third day, just as the Scriptures said. He was seen by Peter and then by

the Twelve. After that, He was seen by more than five hundred of His followers at one time, most of whom are still alive, though some have died. Then He was seen by James and later by all the apostles. Last of all, as though I had been born at the wrong time, I also saw Him."

What is important to notice here is that Jesus was *seen*. After the cross, after the grave, after that first resurrection morning, Jesus was seen and felt and experienced. First, by the few, then by many. His appearance was not the result of some wishful groupthink or delusion or a lie. Jesus was seen—and this was the message of the Church. The gospel without the resurrection was unthinkable for Paul. He was absolutely sure of this one thing—that Jesus was alive.

The story of Jesus does not even end with an empty tomb. The story doesn't end with a few appearances to his followers that changes their lives and futures forever. It does not even end with his ascension into heaven forty days after the resurrection. The story of Jesus actually ends where it began—with glory.

An Eternal Glory

Don't let our tradition of Christmas confuse you. The story of Jesus does not begin in Bethlehem. It does not begin any place or at any time. Jesus had no beginning. (I know, it makes my brain hurt too.)

In that "no beginning," Jesus possessed and enjoyed the same glory as the Father. It's no less than Jesus himself who pulls back the veil of eternity past, when in John 17:5 (MEV), Jesus prayed, *"And now, Father, glorify me in your own presence with the glory that I had with you before the world existed."*

Before the world existed, before time, before space, before the "big bang" of creation when God spoke everything into existence, Jesus was there with the Father and with the Spirit.

Glorious.

Eternal.

Indescribable.

And what was that glory like? Scripture gives us a glimpse.

In Psalm 19:1-2 the Bible tells us:

"The heavens declare the glory of God, and the sky above proclaims his handiwork. Day to day pours out speech, and night to night reveals knowledge."

What King David is telling us here is that hints and clues of God's glory are revealed to us in the physical world and the universe around us. To get a little taste of the glory of God and the glory of Jesus, all you have to do is spend some time looking at the images of deep space that the Hubble Space Telescope has given us. Star after star, galaxy after galaxy all point us to what King David the Psalmist could never have even imagined. The Hubble Telescope has also revealed just how big our universe is as well. It is mind-blowing big. It is inconceivable in its vastness. Surely this is to show us that God and his glory are brighter than anything we could ever conceive or imagine.

This creates a problem. How can infinite glory become finite? How can indescribable and unknowable glory become knowable and visible and personal to where you would want to sit down and invite that glory to come over for dinner—or coffee—or just to hang out together?

An Emptied Glory

That brings us to what we celebrate at Christmas. That brings us to the story of Bethlehem and shepherds and wise men and a manger.

You see, the only way for us to get to God was for him to come to us. And the only way for God to come to us was by a willful act of glorious surrender. He had to give up his glory. He had to step down from that glory with the Father in order to step into our messed-up world. And that meant becoming one of us—in every sense of the word. Jesus became one of us. He moved in with us as a neighbor would move in next door. Except this neighbor was just a baby, a baby just like any other baby, that needed to be nursed and burped and changed.

Paul describes this glorious surrender in Philippians 2:5-8:

"Have this mind among yourselves, which is yours in Christ

Jesus, who though He was in the form of God, did not count equality with God a thing to be grasped, but emptied Himself, by taking the form of a servant, being born in the likeness of men. And being found in human form, He humbled Himself by becoming obedient to the point of death, even death on a cross."

One way to understand how Jesus "emptied himself" is that he emptied himself of the glory he once had with the Father. A glory that was then constrained by the limitations of being flesh and blood just like us. As a result of that surrender, for some 33 years Jesus lived not in glory, but in weakness, in poverty, in pain, and, yes, finally in death.

Don't miss the wonder of what Jesus did. Don't miss the majesty and magnitude of what Jesus had to lay aside. The one whose essence was an indescribable eternal glory became one of us.

It is the great reversal. We spend our lives scratching and clawing our way up …

up the corporate ladder,
up the organizational chart,
up the pay scale,
up the number of Facebook friends,
up the number of Twitter followers.

For Jesus, it was just the opposite. He emptied himself all the way down to the point of death on a cross. Let that sink in for a moment.

Glorious One,
Of Whom creation was made,
It was all for Him and rightfully so,
But gladly allowed His glory to fade
Flesh and blood He became
Look how far down He would go
The Father's love and grace to show

There were moments during his ministry when those around him were given glimpses of his previous glory.

In John 1:14, John tells us:

"And the Word became flesh and dwelt among us, and we have seen His glory, glory as of the only son from the Father, full of grace and truth."

What glory was John referring to here? Perhaps John was referring to the many miracles Jesus performed in front of the disciples. When Jesus turned the water into wine, John refers to that miracle as the first sign where Jesus showed his glory.

Surely what John is referring to above all in John 1:14 was the memory of a mountain top.

We have all heard the cliché about something being a "mountain-top experience," but what James, John, and Peter got to experience was the real deal.

In Mark 9:2-8, there is the account of Jesus taking the

three up a high mountain and being transformed in front of them.

> *"His clothes became radiant, intensely white, as no one on earth could bleach them. And there appeared to them Elijah with Moses, and they were talking with Jesus."*

John surely never forgot that moment and the glory of Jesus there that day. That mountain-top moment would have been seared into his memory. Perhaps it was that moment of glory on the mountain top with Jesus that would later give John the courage to be there with Jesus at the cross.

A Greater Glory

When Jesus was raised from the dead, he was raised not just to life but also to glory. Again, in John 17:5, Jesus prayed that the Father would *"glorify me in your own presence with the glory that I had with you before the world existed."* It was a prayer that the Father answered with the empty tomb.

Then, to the two disciples who met Jesus on the road to Emmaus in Luke 24:26, Jesus said, *"Was it not necessary that the Christ should suffer these things and enter into His glory?"*

Then, there is the promise that Jesus has given us in Mark 13:26 about his return: *"And then they will see the Son of Man coming in clouds with great power and glory."*

Taken together, the clear picture of Scripture is that Jesus, at this very second, as you read these words, has reclaimed that glory he once had with the Father.

Occasionally I will see a bumper sticker that says "My boss is a Jewish carpenter." I understand the thought, but it is not what we have in Jesus. He is no longer just a Jewish carpenter from the backside of nowhere. He is no longer merely the miracle-working Rabbi. He is no longer the Messiah who suffered and died for the sins of the world. No, he is now much more than all of those things. In fact, the case can be made for Jesus now having even greater glory than before.

Consider again what Paul wrote in Philippians 2:9-11:

"Therefore God has highly exalted Him and bestowed on Him the name that is above every name, so that at the name of Jesus every knee should bow, in heaven and on earth and under the earth, and every tongue confess that Jesus Christ is Lord, to the glory of God the Father."

Did you catch that? Do you see what's being described here by Paul? Because of the cross, because of his obedience to the point of death, even death on the cross, God the Father has "highly exalted" him and given him the "name above all names." That sounds like more glory to me. That sounds like the Father has taken Jesus to a whole different level of glory. A level of glory that Jesus didn't have before, and it is all so that Jesus would be given this unique place in all of creation. The place where everyone, in heaven and on earth, will one day bow before Jesus to confess that he is Lord of all.

Dear reader, one day every person who has ever lived—past, present and future—will bow to the glory and authority of Jesus Christ. It's not a question of if, but a question of when. Some will bow in worship and praise as those who have loved and followed Jesus here in this life. Others, however, will bow in fear and trembling, awaiting what will be an eternal separation and punishment. And even though every knee will bow, for many, it will be too late.

Which group will be yours?
Can you really know?
What makes the difference?

You see, bowing to Jesus in worship and praise begins here and now. It begins with bowing your heart and your life in simple faith. A simple faith that turns away from sin and self and turns to Jesus in believing he is who he says he is and will do what he says he will do.

Is that you?

If following Jesus to become more like Jesus has been outside the box for you or maybe you have been confused by all the "churchianity" that you see around you, then I have good news and I have bad news.

The good news is that there is still time for you to make

a change. There is still time for you to repent and believe and follow Jesus. The bad news is that the clock is ticking.

Just the other day I received the news that a good friend had died. He was just 58 years old. No one is promised tomorrow. For you or for me, tomorrow may never come.

So, even as I write these words, I am praying for you dear one. Yes, you, right there. I am praying that, at this very moment, you will put this book down or your e-reader down, and, wherever you are, you will bow your knee and your heart to the great glory of our great God and Savior Jesus Christ. I am praying that with simple, honest faith you would cry out to him to forgive you and save you and help you to follow him. The words are not what's important. Use whatever words make sense to you. The important thing is what's in your heart.

Put down the book.
He is waiting.
He is listening.

Our Glory

Before we finish this journey together, there is one more stop along the way we need to make. There is one more thing I want you to see that I hope will bless you and prepare you for the journey ahead. The Bible makes the amazing promise that we will share in the glory of Jesus. Did you know that? Has anyone ever told you that? Jesus put it like this in John 14:1-3:

"Let not your hearts be troubled. Believe in God, believe also in me. In my Father's house are many rooms. If it were not so, would I have told you that I go to prepare a place for you? And if I go and prepare a place for you, I will come again and will take you to myself, that were I am you may be also."

The promise of Jesus to us is that he is going to prepare a place for us. What kind of place will that be? A place of glory. In fact, that's often how believers refer to heaven— as "glory." A place that is beyond what we can think or imagine.

I wish Jesus would have told us more about what that place is going to be like, but perhaps one reason he didn't is because there are some things that words cannot describe. How do you describe a sunset? How do you describe love? How do you describe being alive? How do you describe chocolate? Go ahead and give it a shot. It is harder than you think. Heaven is like that. Our words fail us. Our words become nonsense and gibberish. Our words fall into nothingness when compared to the glory of our place with Jesus.

As a result, here is what Paul had to say about that glory in Colossians 3:1-4 (NLT):

"Since you have been raised to new life with Christ, set your sights on the realities of heaven, where Christ sits in the place of honor at God's right hand. Think about the things of heaven, not the things of earth. For you died to this life, and your real life is

hidden with Christ in God. And when Christ, who is your life is revealed to the whole world, you will share in all his glory."

Have you ever heard someone say that you can be so heavenly minded that you are no earthly good? Well, it appears that Paul would take exception to that line of thought.

In the passage above, Paul clearly tells us that we are to "think about the things of heaven, not the things of earth." In other words, be heavenly minded. Don't be shy about your desire for heaven. Heaven is not a place for timidity or poverty. I don't believe our desire for heaven can ever be too strong. If anything, it is far too weak. Our problem today is that we get so earthly minded that we are of no heavenly good. We get too bogged down in the mundane of washing clothes, getting to work, chasing after the kids, and taking out the trash to think much or deeply about our future dwelling with God.

Dear reader, when was the last time you dreamed of heaven? When was the last time you looked around you and realized that this is not your real home? You and I were made for so much more.

The reason for being heavenly minded is because heaven is where we will share in the glory of Jesus. And, not just some of that glory. In the passage above, Paul tells us that we will share in *all* the glory of Jesus. Now, that word "all" can only mean one thing—all. Think about that. I hope that one little word just blew your mind.

I love the way C.S. Lewis imagines what our desire for heaven should be like in a little mouse named Reepicheep in his book *The Voyage of the Dawn Treader*. At one point, Reepicheep expresses his desire to get to "Aslan's country" and of that desire he says, "My own plans are made. While I can, I sail east in the Dawn Treader. When she fails me, I paddle east in my coracle. When she sinks, I shall swim east with my four paws. And when I can swim no longer, if I have not reached Aslan's country, or shot over the edge of the world in some vast cataract, I shall sink with my nose to the sunrise."

Would that our desire for heaven be as strong as Reepicheep's desire for "Aslan's country."

There are other passages of Scripture such as 2 Corinthians 4:17 where Paul reminds us that our *"light momentary affliction is preparing for us an eternal weight of glory beyond all comparison."*

And then again in Colossians 1:27 where Paul tells us that it is *"Christ in you, the hope of glory."*

Again and again, we are given this amazing promise that one day we will share in all the glory of Christ.

What will that glory be like? Scripture tells us that it will be the glory of being "like" Christ with a glorified physical body. Scripture tells us that it will be the glory of reigning and ruling with him in his Kingdom. Scripture tells us that it will be the glory of rewards for being faithful. Scripture tells us that it will be the glory of those that we have brought with us through our efforts in sharing the gospel. Scripture also tells us that it will be the glory of finally hearing those words, *"Well done, good and faithful servant."*

Always keep in mind that our glory will never take away from his glory. Rather, I believe it will be just the opposite. Our glory will only add to his glory. The brighter our glory, the brighter his glory. Because then, and only then, will following Jesus to become more like Jesus be made complete. It will be the last stroke of the brush. It will be the last chip of the hammer. It will be the last chapter of our story. At long last we will be *"like him for we will see him as he is."*

When we are finally like him as perfect reflections of his grace, love and mercy, that will be real glory—his glory, perfectly reflected in us. Then and there, we will be able to say along with all creation:

"Worthy is the Lamb who was slain, to receive power and wealth and wisdom and might and honor and glory and blessing."
(Revelation 5:12)

In light of that glory, may we say along with the Psalmist in Psalms 17:15:

"When I awake, I shall be satisfied with your likeness."

Until then, dear friend and fellow traveler, follow Jesus. Stay close to him. Keep him clearly in view. Allow him to lead the way.

And as you follow, ever so closely, may you be covered in the dust of the Rabbi.

The Way of Jesus
Questions for the Journey

Chapter Eight " Jesus and Glory"

Where does the story of Jesus really end?

Why is that important to know?

According to Philippians 2:9-11, "every knee will bow" to the glory of Jesus. Will that be you? How can you be sure?

Colossians 3:1-4 tells us that followers of Jesus will actually share in all the glory of Jesus. How does that make you feel?

Why is there no danger in thinking too much about heaven?

How often do you think about heaven?
What do you look forward to in heaven?

NOTES

The Way of Jesus

1.) Bonhoeffer, Dietrich. *The Cost of Discipleship*. 99. New York: Macmillan Publishing, 1961.

2.) Witkin, Howard "Active Learning." Access Date: Jan. 2017. https://www.aish.com/sp/pg/48885127.html.

3.) C.S. Lewis, *Mere Christianity*. 144. New York: Harper-Collins, *The Complete C.S. Lewis Signature Classics*, 2002.

4.) Hirsch, Alan. "State of the Missional Movement" Access date: March, 2017. https://www.100movements.com/articles/state-of-the-missional-movement-part-1.

5.) Hession, Roy. *The Calvary Road*. 11. Fort Washington, Christian Literature Crusade, 1950.

The Way of Jesus and Community

1.) Harvard Second Generation Study. "Study of Adult Development." Access Date: Jan. 2017. https://www.adultdevelopmentstudy.org/grantandglueckstudy.

The Way of Jesus and Life in the Kingdom

1.) Warren, Rick. *The Purpose Driven Life*. 17. Grand Rapids: Zondervan, 2002.

The Way of Jesus and Mission

1.) Kaiser, Walter C. "The Promise of the Messiah." billygraham/decision-magazine/November-2006/The Promise of the Messiah.

2.) Desiring God. "You Have One Life—Don't Waste It." http://youtube.com/watch?v=mfpmbmsvu3A.

The Way of Jesus and Love

1.) Lewis, C.S. *The Four Loves*. 126. London: Cox & Wyman Ltd., 1960.

The Way of Jesus and Suffering

1.) The Ranch. "I Walked a Mile with Pleasure." Accessed January, 2017. https://theranch.org/2008/02/20/robert-browning-hamilton-i-walked-a-mile-with-pleasure/.

2). C.S. Lewis. *The Problem of Pain*. 604. New York: HarperCollins, *The Complete C.S. Lewis Signature Classics*, 2002.

The Way of Jesus and Glory

1.) Lewis, C.S. *The Voyage of the Dawn Treader*. 231. New York: HarperCollins, 1994.

CPSIA information can be obtained
at www.ICGtesting.com
Printed in the USA
LVHW041220150920
666054LV00003B/233